A Schizophrenic Will

A Story of Madness,
A Story of Hope

By William Jiang, MLS

New York

This is a work of nonfiction. The names and certain
identifying characteristics of many individuals described
in this book have been changed.

None of the passages in this book should be understood
or construed as a recommendation or condemnation of
any particular drug, medication, or treatment for mental
illness.

ISBN-10: 1451512244
ISBN-13: 978-1451512243

Jiang, William, 1972-
A Schizophrenic Will: A Story of Madness, A Story of
Hope

William Jiang
170 p.
l. Jiang, William, 1972-.2. Schizophrenics-United States
Biography

Poetry is the fire of ꞏ
taking the form of w

*Poetry is the fire of my soul,
taking the form of writing.*

A Schizophrenic Will: A Story of Madness, A Story of Hope
By William Jiang, MLS

Acclaim for A Schizophrenic Will

"A talented ambitious young student is afflicted by the most dread mental illness in the prime of his life. This first person account describes this all to common occurrence but what is unique is how he reacts to this adversity and his courageous and successful journey to recovery. Will Jiang's impressive and moving story is reminiscent of other similar first person accounts of personal struggle and triumph over mental illness including Elyn Saks' The Center Cannot Hold and Temple Grandin's Thinking In Pictures: and Other Reports from My Life with Autism. Will's story will be similarly informative and inspirational to everyone who has the good fortune to read it."

Jeffrey Lieberman, M.D.
President, American Psychiatric Association
Lawrence E. Kolb Professor and Chairman
Department of Psychiatry
Columbia University College of Physicians and Surgeons
Director of the New York State Psychiatric Institute

"In "A Schizophrenic Will," William Jiang tells a riveting and compelling story about his struggles with schizophrenia and his emergence at the other end with a good and productive and gratifying professional and personal life. He also gives advice to other consumers, e.g. on navigating college, and who knows better than someone who's lived through it himself? Jiang's story should help people understand what schizophrenia is like and in the process destigmatize an illness that is badly in need of destigmatization."

Elyn Saks, J.D., Ph.D. USC Gould School of Law, Orrin B. Evans Professor of Law, Psychology, and Psychiatry and the Behavioral Sciences. Award Winning Author, The Center Cannot Hold

"With an incredible strength of will William Jiang describes his life dealing with one of the hardest conditions to live with: Schizophrenia. Again and again he fights against the disease and despite all odds secures a professional career and fulfilled life. A must read for any person coping with Schizophrenia, whether you are a sufferer, relative, friend, physician or a scientist working on mental disorders."

Christoph Kellendonk Ph.D.
Assistant Professor of Pharmacology in Psychiatry
Columbia University

"Will Jiang's experiences as detailed in his book are a wonder to read and can help you to understand schizophrenia better. I highly recommend it."

Dan Frey, B.A. Former Editor-in-Chief
New York City Voices, a Journal for Mental Health

"This inspirational story is a great read for anybody, but family and friends of those suffering with schizophrenia will especially find it useful for learning what it is like to live with schizophrenia."

Leaf Jiang, Ph,D., Brother
"William Jiang's extraordinary chronicle of his life is at once arresting, horrifying, challenging and inspiring. Obviously Will Jiang is a brilliant young handsome man born prematurely to an Anglo-Saxon mother and an absentee Russian Jewish father and later adopted by his Chinese stepfather Yu Jiang: the inordinately touching memories of and tributes from his brothers Leaf, Chung and Justice as well as comments introduced in his preface form an impressive list of people attest to the fact that this is a unique young man.

But the reason this autobiography is so deeply moving is the fact that Will Jiang was diagnosed at age 19 as a paranoid schizophrenic and given the fact that he is well educated (has earned a BA and ad Masters of Library Science, speaks four languages, served as the Columbia University/NYSPI Medical Library Chief, and has written a number of fine books), the manner in which he is able to not report as a bystander the workings of the mind sinking into psychotic depths but instead relating to the reader the feeling of that descent , treatment, horrors, and eventual recovery is nothing short of astonishing.

This book takes us by the hand and walks us through the first suggestions of mental illness, plunges us into the moment by moment nightmares that assault the mind of a schizophrenic patient, makes us feel the effects of the medications and treatments, and then beckons us into the light and his own discovery of natural nutritional techniques that help heal the brain. It is an odyssey, reading this book, but it is also a journey lead by a guide who knows each aspect of it well.

Will Jiang writes so well that it is hoped he will embrace his gift for his literary talent and continue writing major works. He is an extraordinary man who is doing more to educate the public about the world of the mentally ill victims while providing a brilliant beacon of hope. Highly Recommended."

Mr. Grady Harp
Amazon Hall of Fame top 100 Reviewer, Vine Voice

TABLE OF CONTENTS

Introduction

By Leaf Jiang, PhD

My older brother, Will, and I have been close throughout our lives. As kids, our aunt described us as two peas in a pod. We played together all the time; whether it was handball, role-playing games, basketball, boxing, play-fighting, or computer games, we had fun and he always included me in his activities with his friends. Will was certainly the pathfinder of this duo, figuring things out and showing me the way. When Will went off to college, I saw how hard he worked -- one (sometimes two) full time jobs with a declared double-major. Before his first breakdown in college, he was 49-chin-up strong, read-more-than-one-book-a-day bright, vibrant, and driven.

The topic of my college entrance essay for MIT was to describe who was the most influential person in my life and how he has shaped me. I wrote about Will and how his work ethic inspired me to work hard and eventually graduated as salutatorian from Stuyvesant High School in New York City, arguably one of the most competitive public high schools in the United States. Even after Will's breakdown, he was a source for inspiration, help, and support. I remember Will getting me my first academic summer job after my freshman year at MIT. He literally walked through NYU's physics department and knocked on all the professors' doors, asking if they needed an intern. I don't think many brothers would do that for each other.

I remember Will after his first breakdown as an undergraduate at Stonybook University and being locked up in their mental ward. The future was uncertain at that time and it wasn't clear if we would ever get Will back. When I visited Will in the ward, he looked like he dropped in weight by 50 lbs, had bruises on his face, and was noticeably uncomfortable. Later, I learned about the paranoid thoughts that lead him there. Even with mind-numbing medication, Will was still able to graduate from college.

It took several years of medication and psychiatric hospital visits before Will figured out what medications and doses worked for him. In the meantime, he earned a masters degree in library science. Excessive thinking, like the thinking that one does when studying or trying to understand complex things, triggers his illness. It is remarkable that he was able to drive himself through school mentally, when all he really could have done was just lie back and let the government checks come in the mail, and when the very act of educating himself was potentially dangerous because it could set off his illness. His masters degree was an admirable achievement.

10

After graduate school, Will became involved with mental health publications (New York City Voices), was the best man at my wedding, and is working as a librarian. We still keep in touch and it always brings a smile to my face when he tells me that I'm not paid what I'm worth. I am proud to be his brother and I hope that you find Will's story inspiring because being a part of it has greatly inspired me.

Chapter 1: How far down does this rabbit hole go?

My brain now needed to work faster. I was taking twenty-three credit hours that included Advanced Physics I, Computer Data Structures, History of the English Language, Chinese, and several other difficult classes. The previous month I had taken 9 credit hours in an intense period that spanned four weeks. The courses included microeconomics, Intermediate French II, and one other class. Was this healthy? Yes, I suppose. But, I soon discovered that my total immersion in academics was a double-edged sword.

That morning I went to the administration building to check up on my attempts to make the government recognize me as a self-supporting adult. To put myself through college, I had been working as a janitor for two years. This was very exhausting in light of the academic load I carried.   I desperately wanted to qualify for federal educational grants so I could continue my studies without having to work as a janitor, scrubbing toilets five days a week. I wanted to be able to concentrate exclusively on my studies.

I remember the financial aid officer's name. When I asked her about the grants and about how much money I would be receiving for the academic year, she replied, "None." I was devastated. It was just like the previous two years. "Your parents make too much money to qualify you to receive financial aid," she explained. I was floored. I told her I had been self-supporting for two years, and I asked her why the school still considered me a dependent. I didn't understand.   I must have expressed some sort of strange reaction because Delores came out from behind the counter to see if I was ok. I assured her that I was fine. That's when the first paranoid thoughts came to my head. They know! They know I've been getting a few thousand each year from mom. They know. I've got to keep quiet about this, I thought. I didn't know who I might have pissed off in the government.

Still reeling, I walked to the Student Union. Despite not qualifying for grant money, I still needed to eat, and I had to sign up for a meal plan. So, I quietly stood in line holding my student lunch form in my hand and waited for my picture to be taken. I remember my feelings of paranoia. With each passing minute, the intensity of the feelings increased, and I was scared. When it was my turn to have my photo taken, the food services woman asked me which meal plan I wanted. It was an easy question, but at that moment, it wasn't simple for me. In my paranoid state, everything had more meaning than it was supposed to. Thinking that she was testing me, I hesitated. She said in a louder, impatient voice, "Which lunch plan do you want to sign up for?" I blurted something out, and I guess it satisfied her. I put on my glasses when they took my picture for the ID so that whoever was after me would not recognize me from behind the light tinted lenses. I remember the look of distraction and fear in my eyes when I later looked at the ID photo. The day was off to a terrible start.

Later that day, I was riding in the car of one of my Chinese friends. A fear of Chinese gangsters suddenly took possession of me. I realize now that I was delusional, but I was convinced that my friends that I had known for two years were Asian gangsters. I also thought they were going to drive me to some isolated spot and put a bullet into my brain. To escape, I would have to act fast and think smart. So, I told them I was not feeling well and to drive me to Stonybrook University Hospital. We were about a mile away, and I felt I would be safe and not be killed by them there. They couldn't trick me to leave the hospital, because I knew if they did, I would die. They would erase me from the pages of life.

At Stonybrook University Hospital, I was quickly admitted, and I was relieved when I was put in a room behind a large steel door with a small glass window. I felt safe. I looked at the clock. It was 4pm. Good. I could get out soon, and go to the police to tell them what was going on with the gangsters who were in league with some sick government plot to take away financial aid from college students. Then I thought, the police? What if some of them were crooked? A journalist for the New York Times would probably be a better choice. It must be an immense conspiracy if the gangsters could actually reach out to Stonybrook.

A teenager who looked like a rebellious, drug user was in the room with me. He had messy hair and wore a black T-shirt with ripped jeans. He began talking to me about his exploits with drugs. I spoke with him for a few moments. But, I wasn't going to try to befriend that guy. No way. I was too cautious about my health to become involved with the subculture of drugs and to expose myself to some awful disease.

There was a quiet guy in the room. I tried to talk to him, but he just remained quiet. I thought that was odd. Eventually, I left him alone. About an hour into the hospitalization I began to relax. Then, staff brought a tall black guy into the room. He was a scary dude. Why was he scary? He just stood in the middle of the room and jerked his body around while standing in the same place. His clothes were a mess-- all wet. And after a few more minutes he started to shake violently and got an erection that was clearly visible through his wet sweatpants. This guy just totally grossed me out. Two guards in

13

red blazers put on latex gloves and subdued him, and they led him out of the room. I was wondering why they would allow a guy like that in the same room with people like me. I actually had no idea where I was. I didn't know I was in a psychiatric emergency room. I thought I was just in a waiting room. Another hour went by, and I went to lie down in one of the rooms to rest. In the room was a swarthy looking guy. He had dark hair and olive skin, Latino. We struck up a conversation about Cervantes "Don Quixote". He told me he worked as a literature professor at Stonybrook University. I was impressed. I have always been impressed by people who are knowledgeable. We talked about the sadness and the futility of Don Quixote's dream. The fact that he chose to chase that impossible star was both sad and at the same time noble, we agreed. That the man of La Mancha could lead such a life of delusion and nobility seemed to be a contradiction to me, I remember. I think, in retrospect, that I, too, have been fighting windmills my entire life.

After a while, I went back into the main reception area. They had brought in a cute, little Japanese girl. I was attracted to her; however, I thought of myself as a "taken" man. I had a girl in my life that I possibly wanted to marry. My love interest was my girlfriend since high school. I was the kind of guy that would allow his eyes to wander and allow himself to talk to other girls, but I would never be unfaithful. I loved her too much. So, I sat in the reception area without saying anything, for a while. The Japanese girl was sitting next to the quiet guy. Naturally, I thought they were together. Eventually, I talked to the girl, and I asked her if she was with him. She said no. I thought they were sitting too close for them not to know each other. That was strange. Then, while we were talking, she started looking at me with eyes full of lust. Her gaze made me uncomfortable. She stopped talking to me and just started looking at me while sucking on one of her fingers in a very sensual manner. We stopped talking. She stared at me, sucking on her finger for awhile. I felt I had to say something. I told her that I wasn't interested in her because I already had a girlfriend. She told me that she didn't care. She just kept looking at me and sucking on her finger. It was sickening. At that point in my life, I considered myself good-looking, but this was ridiculous. I thought, this girl must be a nymphomaniac, the way she was acting. No way I'm getting involved with her. Not only do I not want to cheat on my girlfriend, but I concluded that this girl probably has a bunch of sexually transmitted diseases.

I looked at the clock. Everything changed for me at that moment. I knew I had been there for hours already, but the time still said four pm. I stared again at the clock. The little hand was on the four and the big hand was on the twelve. I

started to put two and two together. It was four pm when I
came in, and now it was still four? These people aren't here
to help me. They are here to keep me trapped. They're here
to take away my freedom! They're in league with the government. Damn! I've fallen into one of their cells behind a locked
door where I can't get out. I walked towards the exit. A
security guy in a red blazer told me in a loud voice to get away
from the door. This is ridiculous, I thought. I'm an American!
How can these people keep me against my will? I have broken
no laws. I have hurt no one!

I felt that this must be how Jesus felt. Jesus was wrongly
persecuted in his life. Just as I am being persecuted. I could
have been a drug dealer many times in my life, picked up a
gun and settled a few scores, or just become some kind of
loser. I could have become someone with no future who didn't
try. I could have been someone who didn't work hard, as a
janitor to pay their way through college.   I've had a hard life,
I thought. I don't deserve to be treated this way. It's not
right. But, Jesus forgave his enemies. And so will I. Because
I thought I knew exactly how Jesus felt, I reasoned, I must be
an incarnation of Jesus.

Images flew through my mind. There was an excellent movie
called Amadeus which chronicled a possible but far-fetched
theory that Amadeus Wolfgang Mozart may have been mur-
dered by Salieri, a musical competitor of Mozart. At the end of
the movie, after Salieri confesses to his role in the demise of
Mozart, the priest looked shocked to find a heart so black. The
scene cuts to Salieri being lead through the mental asylum,
absolving his fellow inmates. "I absolve you" "I absolve you"
he repeated to everyone he saw. He said this to the people
in cages and the people in chains. He laughs an evil laugh
and says, "I absolve everybody." And the movie ends, and the
credits roll. For some reason, this aspect of the movie Amadeus went through my mind the same instant I thought I was
some kind of incarnation of Jesus. I, think that I, being a better person than Salieri, could truly absolve people. I think that
people will recognize my goodness and feel better about being
where they were. I walk around the room saying "I absolve
you" to people who are there.   What happened next, I did not
expect.

I saw a lot of activity behind the glass enclosure of the
room where most of the people wearing white were. Two big
men wearing white come out of the room where the doctors
and nurses are. I braced myself, not knowing what to expect.
Others dressed in white at the same time charged me from
behind the glass enclosure. I was quickly surrounded by six
men, and the two big guys rapidly grabbed each of my arms

and a third was at my back with what felt like a gun. They led me to a room where I was sure I was going to die. I was sure they were going to kill me. I was kicking and screaming at this point.

"Let me go!" I screamed. In the room, I saw a gurney. They dragged me to it. I was not strong enough to resist all the hands. There were too many of them. After they got me on the gurney, they covered my head and I was enveloped in darkness. At that moment, I thought of a sick movie I had seen about two years earlier called "Faces of Death" where some devil worshippers supposedly were having a filmed orgy of death. This thought intensified the terror I felt. Were they going to eat me alive? I wouldn't let it happen! I struggled and struggled to no avail. I was a lamb and I was certain that they were taking me to the slaughter. It all made sense. This wasn't some kind of government conspiracy. This was a conspiracy of Satan. No wonder it could persist so long and so secretively. After what seemed to be an eternity, I was on my back in some kind of strait-jacket. Down the middle of the straight jacket was "No!" written at least twenty times. What the hell were these people doing? I vowed that they could kill me, but I'd never become one of them. I feared the consequences of not giving into their infernal power.

I heard giggling. I saw children in the room, three little girls. I was shocked. How could these people do these unnatural acts in front of children, I thought? The children were laughing and playing, oblivious to my fate. They looked at me, just as the adults did, with soulless, hungry eyes. These children must be the spawn of Satan. The mix of their innocence with their evilness was horrifying to my core.
As I struggled and yelled. "Why can't someone help me?" One of the men in red jackets who was holding my head between his hands, restraining me, said, "We are trying to help you." Yes, I know, I thought. Satan is the father of lies, and this devil is lying as well. Why doesn't he just crack my neck and end my suffering? It would be the humane thing to do. No. They all want me to suffer. They want me to re-nounce good. It will not happen, even though I'm an atheist. I thought, I had no idea these forces were at play on my very campus of Stonybrook University. Wait until I get out, and let the world know what is going on in this hospital. Sick! This ward is just a front for a sick secret society. Then, I wonder how many people outside of this hospital are actors who help these sick people to trap people in this diabolic place.

The men and women in white coats who were some kind of medical staff left eventually, even the red-coated guard that I was hoping would crack my neck. But, the little girls stayed.

16

As time passed I watch them play on the white institutional floor of my room. They seem like normal little girls, but I could tell that there is something different about them. Something was not right about them. Finally, after being confined to that straight jacket for what seemed to be an eternity, a man who looked like a giant, about seven feet tall, and a man in a red jacket took me out of my restraints and off the gurney. They walked me to the door that I had entered when I came to this place. My heart leaped, although my head felt heavy somehow. Maybe they were going to let me go! They opened the heavy, metal door. Then, they opened another heavy metal door behind that one. I can't run because they're holding on my arms. The second door opens, and I see…My family! How could they be here? They are supposed to be in Manhattan! My God! What's going on?!? Why are they here? Are we all going to die as a family?! "Noooooooooo!" my mind yelled. But, it was muted. They must have injected me with something. Strangely, these men don't seem to bother with my family. Nobody in my family was being restrained. I was lead towards them. Their faces, I couldn't read. My family: Mom, Dad, Leaf are just standing there. I didn't understand. Are they in league with the Devil? Why aren't they doing anything to help me? Am I just some kind of living medical experiment? What's going on? I'm dragged away to an elevator. And I go up. I'm barely conscious of what is going on. The last thing I remember is seeing the number to the door of my room: 1010. Great, I'm going to be just another story on the NYC radio station 1010 WINS tomorrow. Just another statistic. My death will be made to seem as if it were an accident. I'm sure.

The next two days are a dark blur-- literally. I remember shadow encompassing everything, darkness everywhere I looked. Some pinhole points of light poked through the dark walls of my reality. But, what enveloped me was darkness, everywhere. The first thing I can remember is a nurse telling me that I was going to be presented to "The Team". I had no idea what to make of this. I thought, maybe if I tell a good enough lie, they'll forgive me and let me go. So, I waited in a chair until being summoned into a large room with maybe fifteen people in white coats.

"Why are you here?" One of the doctors asked me.
I lied. "I took some red pills. Speed," I said. "I guess it got me wired up. I took them to do well on an exam."
"There were no traces of drugs in your urine," said the doctor.
I was trapped in a lie. Unless I could think faster than these exquisite liars, I'd be here for a long time, I thought. But, I knew you can't out-lie the infernal. So, I remained silent.
The doctor continued, "Speed comes in red pills, but we

couldn't find any traces of drugs in your system."

I stood there, silent. Looking at me, their infernal eyes burned into my head.

I was asked a bunch of other questions. I can't recall what they asked. Ultimately, I was led out of the room. I was relieved to get away from them. Looking back, yes. Amphetamines, affect the dopamine in the brain, as do many of the street drugs. I wasn't wired up on speed. I was naturally high. I studied and worked so hard those two years I was at Stonybrook, I guess something snapped.

I learned later that there is something called the dopaminergic theory of schizophrenia. It posits that the excitatory neurotransmitter has something to do with schizophrenia. The older drugs, block dopamine in the brain. They have the opposite effect of many street drugs. On cocaine, I understand, you feel really, really good. I felt really, really good naturally. The higher the dose of the antipsychotic drugs one takes, the worse one feels. This is precisely because of the effect of the drugs on the pleasure/reward center of the brain.

At one point, in the darkness of my first few days of hospitalization, I remember that I was in a medium-sized room with a lot of chairs, arranged for a group meeting. Some of the people in the room wore white coats, some didn't. I remembered the people in white coats downstairs were the devil's people. They terrified me with their occasional fake smiles and hungry eyes. I remember the "doctors" were going around the room asking people why they thought they were here. It had to be a trick. It was a trick to weed out the strong from the weak, the wheat from the chaff. They were preparing to reap souls. I was sure. I felt that I had to try to show that I was strong enough to survive by showing I could be insensitive and strong.

I waited until the thoughts that were racing through my mind started to settle, and I noticed easy prey. A middle-aged Caucasian woman in the group talked with difficulty for a while about the reasons she was there: her husband was dead and she was depressed. She talked through sobs, and it broke my heart to see and hear her. However, as soon as I could, I jumped on the chance to get out of there by mocking her and the death of her husband. I called her weak. I would do anything at this point to get out of the pit of hell in which I was trapped. I would do things I never thought I ever would. The "doctors" looked at me in a way that said to me, you will be here for a long time. I remember the woman cried. What the hell was I supposed to do to get out of this place? Dammit! I felt bad because the woman was crying. But, I couldn't ask her to forgive me. That would show that I was weak to the devil worshippers. And I knew what happens to the weak around Satan.

That's the only scenario that I remember clearly from the beginning of my hospitalization. I lost track of time. Days went by, and the next thing I knew, I wake up in a bed that is not my dorm room bed at Stonybrook University. My back hurts, and I groggily sit up. I realize I'm sitting on a gurney, and everything that happened in the emergency room comes rushing back to me like a horror movie with me as the subject of the movie. And, I think, I know what they do to the main characters of these horror movies. Sometimes it takes a little while, sometimes a long while, but eventually they die.

So, I got up, and looked around my room. Feet dangling from the gurney and wearing a hospital gown, I noticed that the gurney I was sleeping on had its back elevated. That explains the sore back, I thought. Then, I noticed the gurney was facing the window that had the morning light from the heavens streaming in like all of glory. That morning light was a reminder for me of all that was good in my life: my mother, my father, my brothers: Leaf, Chung, Justice, my lover, and the kind of life I was living. I was pure of body and mind. I didn't do drugs or commit crimes, and I was an extremely hard worker of body and mind. I took that realization to my heart and kept it there because I was sure I would need it.

There were two doors in my room. An institutional blue door was in front of me. It was closed. There was a door to my right. The door to the right was halfway open, and it was noisy on the other side of it. But, I wanted to explore my room so I could see what I was dealing with here. I noticed air vents near the bottom of the wall near a door, and I noticed the faint smell of sulphur in the air. It made sense these people would give me this environment. They wanted to remind me of their allegiance to Satan, so how better could they remind me of that than give me smells from hell: fire and brimstone, the brimstone being the odor of sulphur that was permeating my room.

I easily lifted myself from my gurney with my strong arms. I took in the rest of the room while I sprung to the ground and felt the cold floor beneath my bare feet. The room was painted white, all white, depressingly white. There was a square window to the left of my bed from which the good light was streaming through with a warm, life-sustaining, yellow hue. There was a wooden dresser and a large, blue, plastic chair. The floor was made with institutional white tiles, the kind I had cleaned in the hallways of the first floor of the Social and

Behavioral Sciences building as a janitor while going to school.

I felt the need to go to the bathroom. I figured there was too much noise coming from the door to the right to be a bathroom, so I walked straight to the door in front of me. I opened the door. It was my bathroom. It was small. It had a polished metal mirror, a toilet, a white tile floor, a shower, and another institutionally-painted blue door. I guess I'm sharing my bathroom. How pleasant. I started to make use of the toilet by urinating. I heard and felt a demonic presence in the room. Because of the demonic presence, I understood that I would have to control everything I did in this place, everything down to my urination. Because going to the bathroom is a release, and a release is a sort of pleasure, I did so at my life's peril. I'd better keep things Spartan, I told myself. I quickly finished my business and got out of the bathroom.

After leaving the bathroom, I decided to check out what was beyond the other door. I opened it. What I saw was very strange. There were people in the hallway, but they weren't moving. They were standing in mid-stride, as statues do. The hallway was half dark-half light, and one of the lights flickered. The hall was full of institutional furniture, and it looked very much like a normal hospital. I walked up to a wooden desk with large binders behind it. I immediately saw my name written on one of the binders, and I thought about what this could mean.

In the Middle Ages, passion plays were done to teach and remind the people inhabiting the English countryside of the dead seriousness of taking their religion deep into the core of their beings. I recalled my Medieval English Literature class the previous semester and a passion play called "Everyman". In this play, the main character is called "Everyman". The play is an allegorical story where things are labeled with what they are supposed to represent. Everyman represents every man and every woman. His journey in the play represents everyone's quest for what is necessary to get to heaven. To make a long story short, there was a book in the play. It was the book that contained the good and bad deeds of "Everyman". I knew immediately that the binder with my name on it was my book of deeds. I realized that this was to be the place I would be judged.

Bewildered, I stumbled back into my room and walked to the window to be in the warm yellow light. The pure light. The problem was that the light was emanating from outside the hospital. Yes, I was in the light. But, the light was in the hospital, and I was trapped in the hospital. I got on my knees and bowed my head while I stayed in the light. I knew that I would need to be strong here, stronger that I had ever been. I whispered under my breath an atheist's prayer, whatever the hell that is.

Chapter 2: A Trying Time in a Young Life, Stony Brook Hospital, Room 1010

One of the first memories I have of being locked up in the ward was of the eye of Satan. Well, that's what I thought the setting sun was when I was behind those walls. Let me explain. Usually, during the day the sun has a cheerful yellow glow. While the sun is setting, sometimes, it is almost the color of blood. It is certainly red. So, everyday after having that thought, I feared the setting of the sun and the coming of night. Night, especially midnight, was horrifying to me. They call midnight "the witching hour" in some books. The longer I stayed in the hospital, the more I believed in those tales of dark magic. The next day would confirm my fears. I woke up, and eventually got to "The bubble Room" where the newspapers were. There was a newspaper screaming, in large bold letters, about the Los Angeles Riots. I was shocked. Insanity inside these walls, and outside as well! The world becoming an asylum for all, I thought.

Looking back at my first hospitalization, one event in particular stands out for me in retrospect. It is the memory of confronting a seven-foot tall psychiatric nurse. Call me crazy, but anyone who has the guts to aggressively confront a guy almost a foot taller than themselves, unarmed is clearly on another planet. Bob was his name. I remember that situation well. I was in my room, seething that the demons and devils were keeping me locked up. I tried to change my state of mind by imagining my mind and heart as blocks of steel, so I would not be afraid of them. But, every noise outside my door made me jump because the thought came that it was uncertain when the Devil's spawn would tire of playing this game of cat and mouse, me being the mouse?

I felt the need to feel pain to harden my resolve, good, purifying pain. So, I looked around my small room. There was not much there to hurt myself with. A gurney and a large wooden dresser. I checked the bathroom for a glass mirror. No. The mirror was of highly polished metal, and the toilet couldn't be budged. So, I went to my door and I closed it ever so gingerly so that no one would notice and stop me from my endeavor, and I walked over to the dresser. It was so heavy that I couldn't really lift it; however, I was able to tip it. So, I tipped it onto my foot to feel the pain. And, feel it I did. I kept the dresser balanced on my foot for about a minute, and the pain was there. But, not enough. So, I went to the gurney, and thought a bit about how to use it best to get the pain I needed to clear my mind. I got on the floor and rolled the gurney over my left hand. Yes, there was pain. But, neither the gurney going over my hand nor the heavy dresser on my foot hurt enough to make me get outside of my fears.

21

So, I walked outside of my room. The hallway was well-lit and clean. White floor, white walls. People who were obviously lost souls walked in the hall with shambling gaits. The lesser devils and greater devils who kept me locked in here stood and sat behind a long wooden desk. No matter. I saw two women carrying laundry quickly produce a key, unlock the heavy metal and glass door to my left, and quickly get to the other side. I felt that it would be easy to overpower one of these little women to get my freedom, a bit too easy. I had to prove my courage to myself and not pick on the weak. So, I walked around the figure eight unit until I saw Bob produce his keys and move towards the exit.

Bob was a massive man. He was thin, but not rail thin. Healthy, and wiry thin he was. I remember him telling me later that he measured 6'10" in height. So, as soon as I saw him produce the keys, I came after him. He saw my aggressive moves, and bellowed: "Stay!" I was transfixed. I couldn't move. It was like he could just command my mind with magic. I stood in the spot outside the heavy metal and glass doors, beyond which lay my freedom, for what seemed like an eternity, unmoving. "Code M, ten north, Code M ten north" I heard blaring on the intercom. Still transfixed, I saw four burly guys about my size, in red coats, hurry towards me. They wore latex gloves. They grabbed me, hard. Each one took a limb, and they hoisted me into the air. While I struggled, suspended in the air, they carried me to my room where they strapped me to my bed. Those damn leather restraints didn't exactly feel like satin and silk. Then, when I was tied down, a male nurse came over and asked me what I was doing. I knew that he knew, so I didn't answer. He looked at my right hand's ring finger where the gold ring that my mother gave me for my graduation from high school was. He said to me, "We're going to have to take that away." So, I clenched my fist.

No way was I going to let them touch anything my beloved mother gave me, especially this ring. To me, it symbolized my independence, pride, and mother's love. So, the nurse used his two hands to force my hand open. He grabbed my thumb and pulled it back until it seemed like he was going to break it. He bent it all the way back. "Stop!" I screamed. So, he said "About that ring." I had no choice. If my thumbs were broken I couldn't defend myself against anyone. So, the nurse took out some hand lotion, and twisted and turned the ring until eventually he was able to slip it off my finger. Damn him. "You can get it back when you are discharged." He said. I knew he was lying. I knew I was going to die here. Probably in my bed. Damn him. After the excitement I caused had died down. I was still strapped to the bed and couldn't get up. There was a nurse placed outside of my room to keep me under observation. Of course I didn't know that at the time, I just thought she was another infernal worker who was guarding me until her master would do with me as he wished.

Looking back at that entire situation, I realize that my going after the giant psychiatric nurse Bob in that situation is exactly what I've been doing my entire life. I've never taken the easy road when something of principle was at stake. At university I always took the most difficult classes to prove my mental vigor. I've never preyed on the weak because everyone is weak at some point in their life. I've always risen to ethical challenges. When possible, I was always there as someone who cared, if not in word, than in deed, when power was placed in my own two hands. I've nurtured my younger brothers as a father would, and I've been there for my friends as if they were brothers.

From the little window in my room, I could tell that I was high up. I was on the tenth floor of a massive building. I thought I could just tie together a bunch of sheets and rappel down the side of the building, and then I'd be free. So, I tied together about fifty sheets, and I tried to break the window to my room. The glass would not break. I guess I was making a lot of noise. Staff found out what I was doing. I was placed in restraints for roughly an hour or so after that. I hated those restraints. But, the staff was just trying their best to keep me from hurting myself.

Another memory stands out in my mind. I used to be quite a strong youth, but the strength of insanity..well add that to an already strong young male, and that's an entirely different story. One of the days I was in the hospital, I remember, for some reason, I ripped the headboard off of my gurney. Then, I fell to my knees at the window and started to pray in the light that was streaming into my room. The pure light. I wanted the light to fill my being to protect me from the evil I felt was around me. Don't ask me why I ripped the headboard off of my gurney. I have no idea to this day. However, I do remember the staff's reaction when they saw it happened. I was still at the window praying to be let out of that unholy place, and I heard a heavy tread come into the room. I heard, "Holy shit! This guy ripped the headboard off of his gurney!" There was a trace of fear in his voice, I thought. I continued, head down, to pray, waiting to be punished for my transgression on the property of the Devil. However, nothing happened. Some infernal ones that were posing as doctors came into the room. They asked me some questions, I answered. Nothing more became of that situation.

***

Leaf was supposed to be here an hour ago, I told myself. My brother, Leaf, was a high school student and he was coming to visit me at Stonybrook University Hospital that day. I remember thinking that he must have been killed by the same bastards that were keeping me at the hospital. So, I went ballistic. Nobody messes with anyone in my family! The rest of what happened after that is a blur. The speakers blared "Code M. 10 North" and people in white coats rushed around. The next thing I recall is being tied down again. Again the leather restraints. Not good. About four hours later, I saw mom with dad. I thought that Dad had obviously pissed in his pants, he was so scared. He had a big wet mark on his butt. They told me that Leaf was safe, and not to worry. Tension eased away from me. Thank God Leaf was alright, I thought. Mom and Dad stayed for a while. Mom talked a bit about me fighting my dragons. Damn, I knew there were devils and demons here, but I hadn't seen any dragons. I wondered what they looked like.

***

At 5pm every day, the love of my life came to visit me. No matter how badly I felt that day, seeing her brought lightness to my heart. I lived to see her sweet smile and taste her sweet kisses. We had been going out for three and a half years, since high school. She would come with delicious, home-cooked Chinese food. Or fruit. Or flowers. Or stuff to read. Today, she sang to me. She had the sweetest singing voice. This one male nurse that I couldn't stand, complimented her on her beautiful voice. I smiled because she was mine. She was my biggest reason to stay alive and keep hope alive. So, she sang Chinese folk songs to me. Beautiful. I couldn't tell what the words meant. Days melded together until it became a predictable pattern and I had lost sense of time. That kind of thing can happen in a ward that is sterile white.

I thought that the infernal power had absolute power over this realm. So, I had to expel any kind of wanton notions from my head. I controlled my thoughts. I controlled my bodily functions, to the point that I would eat only three apples per day. I did this for two weeks. My weight went from a thin 185 to meager 165. For a guy that is 6'2" that normally eats well over 2,000 calories per day, it was very difficult to subsist on about 300 calories per day.

I remember I volunteered for "cleanup" on the ward. What I had to do for this job was help clean up after the messes made by the other patients after they had eaten in the cafeteria. I would sit in the sun, feeling very hungry, while every-one else ate. It was a very difficult job. Some people there made messes that smelled so good, because I was so hungry. I remember cleaning up some applesauce that someone had dropped on the floor. The fragrant, sweet-smelling, apply goodness permeated my nostrils. But, I just cleaned it up, and cleaned up the other messes. I wiped down the tables, and went back to my room to sit in my big blue plastic chair. I thought I had to control my animalistic bodily functions because things of the body are not of God, and gluttony is one of the seven deadly sins. I wanted to be on God's side.

My room was my refuge. The door was always slightly ajar. If it was open too wide, I was made uncomfortable by the infernal noises outside my room, and when it was totally closed.. Well, I was uncomfortable about being alone with that infernal presence. So, I sat in the blue, plastic chair. For a time, in the beginning of the hospitalization, I'd sit in the chair and stare at the wall opposite me. I imagined that was where my body would be placed after I was killed by these horrid devil-worshiping pretenders. I must have stared at that blank, white wall at least four hundred hours in the month and a half I was there. My mind spun and spun and worked and worked. I didn't know it at the time, but the hospital was the best place for me at that time. It gave me a chance to get myself together. This was a chance I wouldn't have had outside the walls of the ward.

My love brought me apples and flowers. I asked her to bring me apples because they weren't very acidic, and they were more suitable for eating on an empty stomach. I ate the fruit slowly over two weeks, only three apples per day. The flowers were symbolic of our love. I knew they would die on the ward if I was there long enough. So, to remember her kindness I took one of the blossoms and pressed it into a book. I still have that blossom, in one of my photo albums. What the blossom would signify would change as our lives changed. When she gave me the flower, it was alive, like our love. Now it is a dead flower, pressed behind some cellophane, a reminder of what was once a living, beautiful thing. It is still beautiful, but dead. This is also what happened to our love.

***

One of the nurses must have told my love that I wasn't eating much. So, she cooked me some delicious, thick, rice noodles, the next day. She brought the food in a Tupperware container. When she took off the top, the room was filled with the enticing aroma of delicious food. I told her I couldn't eat it. I feared for her safety. I felt if I indulged in this food, she could get hurt by those who would do harm to her. To us. She convinced me to take a small bite. I figured it would be fine. It wasn't. After two weeks of eating only apples. To have this delicious food on the tip of my tongue suffused my senses. It was more than I could bear. I couldn't stop eating, and I ate the entire container full of rice noodles. She seemed very happy. After I saw no harm came to her or to me, I too was happy. She stayed for another hour, and she left. Her warmth was replaced by the cold, diabolic feel of the ward. Somebody screamed. I didn't know what to think. I went to sit in my big blue chair, and I stared at the wall. I sat in the chair, and eventually, the sun set. I glanced at the sun as it went down. The reddish hues it gave off filled my room. Then darkness, the friend of the infernal. I waited there until I felt sleepy. I slept.

Another day, I realized that the biggest thing I could hurt myself with on the unit was a dining room table. Maybe I could get creative with pain if I could get one of those tables to fall on me. I thought it was a good idea. I opened my door, and I strode down the hallway. People got out of my way. Standing at 6'2", nothing but muscle and bone, with a steely look in my eye, well, I'd be afraid of me when I get into that mindset. So, I walked into the dining room, and there was no one there. Good. I got on my back under one of the large tables, and I kicked the end of the table into the air. I forget what happened next. But, the next thing I knew, I was on my bed with a bunch of doctors and nurses around me.

One of the doctors introduced himself. "Hello, I'm Dr. Bush." He said. Great, this Indian guy mocks me as well. He expects me to believe that he's the President of the United States. I don't think so. This is what I thought. I was terrified of the hungry eyes that all the doctors and nurses had on their faces. I was afraid of what they'd do next. I was strapped down and helpless to resist. Dr. Bush pulled out a needle and said, "This won't hurt a bit." He took my blood. For refreshment? Damn blood-sucking spawns of the devil! After an eternity, he said, "There. Done." And, I was lying on the gurney that was soaked in my own blood. Bloody good job, Doc.

***

I'd see the cute nymphomaniac Japanese girl from the Psych Emergency Room around the hospital ward from time to time. I didn't know what to make of her. She always looked at me with eyes full of lust. Nevertheless, I wasn't about to cheat on the love of my life, so I always walked on by. I remember one of the afternoons maybe a week into my hospitalization, I was in bed, trying to relax. I saw a shape come into the room. I pulled up my covers, and there was the Japanese girl. "What are you doing in my room?" I asked. She didn't answer, but instead she tried to climb into bed with me. I just reacted. I got her out of my bed, and yelled at her. "Do not try to get into my bed again, and get out of my room!" She didn't expect that, I don't think. And, she ran out of my room, spurned. I didn't even try to acknowledge her existence after that. In retrospect, maybe I should have been a bit more gentle, but when you're hospitalized for a mental disorder and you're in an acutely disturbed phase, it's hard to give a measured response.

My doctor, Dr. Frances, was a trip. In many older movies the actor depicts the devil sporting a goatee and devilish mustache. I don't know how else to describe him. Well, that's the way he had his facial hair. The first time I saw Dr. Frances was eerie. I thought, this must be Mephistopheles himself. He'd pop up all over the ward, looking for me in unexpected places and situations. One time, I was in a group that was making butter-garlic noodles. He came out of nowhere asked me questions rapidfire. It was really hard to deal with this. I don't recall seeing him often. I think I saw him on average once per day during morning rounds.

Medicine. Central to any experience in a psychiatric hospital these days is medicine. I don't know what they used on me in the Emergency Room. They injected me with something, and they gave me little white pills, later I learned they were called Ativan. The Ativan calmed me down some, but the injected stuff was like a rush of darkness that enveloped me. On the unit, they gave me a liquid to drink. They mixed that foul-tasting stuff with orange juice. The doctors seemed reasonably pleased with it. I wasn't because it caused a red rash to grow on me. The doctors wanted to draw on me with a magic marker to track the rash's growth. I told them I didn't want that to happen, and that I think that the medicine is causing the rash. So, they took me off that medicine, and they started me on another. It was called Navane. The first night I took the Navane, I noticed ghouls were walking outside my door. I couldn't sleep for a long time. Eventually, somehow, I slept. I woke up to a vibration coming from the radiator at the foot of my bed. It was almost painful, and I certainly couldn't sleep. The vibrations came from the air vent. And, I had a painful muscular contraction in my back. "Great." I thought. "This new medicine is going to be worse than the other." So began the day.

After being awoken by the vibrations, I decided I should go do my morning toilet, devil worshipers be damned. So, I went to my bathroom and relieved myself. I brushed my teeth, and

I took a shower. The shower was really the only pleasurable thing I let myself do. Mother used to call that sensation of relaxation "The Angel of the Water". And, really, I needed some of that angelic power these days. The shower was over too quickly. I stepped out of it, and I saw a small pool of water on the floor. "Damn them." I thought. And, I went back to my room. I got dressed. Mom had brought me a pair of shorts with skulls on it. I still have some courage, I thought, but I'd never have the guts to wear skulls around these infernal people, so I got dressed in some fatigues and a t-shirt. Fatigues are the standard issue pants for Army grunts. They're the pants with camouflage print. I thought they were cool back then, even though I knew war is hell. "Hey, I'm in hell." I thought, so there wasn't much of a point in not wearing them. Then I went to the nurses' station to ask for a razor. The nurse acted like I was asking for something unreasonable, but eventually I got my hospital-issue razor. I think someone watched me while I used it. I can't remember. Then, I returned it. The razors they use on psych wards are nothing like a Mach 3. You get lots of nicks. They draw quite a bit of blood. Not a good thing. Then, I waited in my big, blue plastic chair, fearing that I'd be taken out of my room, forcibly, and held down and eaten alive. That was the daily thought, the thought that was ever-present. But, about 8am, a nurse came around with some more liquid Navane. She was a happy person. Her name was Mary. Like the mother of Jesus, I thought. She has to be good. So, I took the proffered medicine, and she smiled. It was rare to see a smile in that place, so I was happy to see it. I responded to the kindness. Then, I went back to the chair, and waited. At 9am, breakfast was served. I had oatmeal, milk, and orange juice. It was the default breakfast. I learned that day, from one of the patients that you could actually pick your own breakfast. So, I did from then on. I also picked my lunches and dinners. It was a nice thing to be able to control what went into your body.

During morning rounds, the doctors asked me a bunch of questions. "How are you?" One asked. That question was asked every day. I felt if I could answer it correctly, I could get out. So, I answered, "I am well. I am sick. I am here, and I am nowhere. I'm a good man. Please let me out." They always took notes, and conferred with each other. But, I never knew what they were thinking. So, I told them, "I don't need medicine." Just like that. And, they surprised me by saying, "Ok, you won't get any tonight, and we'll see how you do."

I was ecstatic. "No medicine!" I thought to myself. I went through the day scared as usual, but happy as a clam. That night, I wasn't offered any Navane. I got into bed. I waited for sleep to overtake me. However, the ghosts, the devils, and the demons outside my door seemed even more menacing than usual. More present. For four hours, I heard people scream-ing, laughing, and shuffling around. Some of the people actu-ally started seeming ethereal. Then, it was like it was in the psych emergency room. The fear was right there, in my face, in my room, in my head. I came to the realization that I was to die tonight. So, I thought to myself, maybe medicine could dull me so I don't have feel this way.

I went up to a doctor and begged him to give me medi-cine. He asked me why. I told him that in Joseph Conrad's book Heart of Darkness, before the main character died, his last words were "Oh, the horror!" I know what he was think-ing now. For me right now, the way I feel is, "Oh the horror! Oh the terror!" Please give me some medicine. He did. I got it. I couldn't sleep until much later, but I think I got one or two hours of sleep. After approximately an hour, the terror had dissipated somewhat. I knew, from that point on, that I would need to keep taking the medicine to keep those feelings of horror and terror at bay. This insight was essential for my eventual recovery.

***

I remember one of the days that melded into the others when I was at 10 North at Stonybrook University Hospital. I was wandering around the ward aimlessly, and I noticed a pamphlet on a shelf titled "Schizophrenia". Out of curiosity I picked it up and read it from cover to cover. There was one passage in there that said "Sometimes people with schizophre-nia think they are Jesus." I thought to myself, hey that hap-pened to me! Maybe I have this disease called schizophrenia. A seed was planted in my mind. Maybe this experience I was having had a name. If it has a name, maybe it can be dealt with and treated!

Anybody who knows the life of the ward, knows that you need to go to groups to hasten getting out of the hospital. I had no idea, so for the first two weeks, I stayed in my room, and I didn't go to groups. It was really difficult to just sit there all day every day, but eventually I figured out the life of the ward. I didn't feel like going to crafts groups, because I had a huge amount of work I needed to do for school: physics, advanced data structures and whatnot, or so I thought. But, to crafts groups, I went. Eventually, I went to every single type of occupational and recreational therapy group I could. It was better than being alone with my demons. At least this way, I was among them.

What is it about psychiatric hospitals and making ashtrays? I think this is something every psych patient has made at one point or another in their lives. A little grout, tile, and an ashtray never seemed so meaningful! In group, I made mine as well. On mine, I even had two heart-shaped tiles, one symbolizing my mother and one symbolizing my love. It was a work of transcendent love. I don't think I could have sold it for all the money in the world, back then. It held too much symbolic sway in my mind. I think I entrusted it to my mother, and it was probably lost in the first few days of giving it to her. It's funny how things become so meaningful when you're in the throes of a nervous breakdown.

At pretty much every psychiatric hospital are community meetings. They happen so patients can voice their concerns and connect with each other and staff in a constructive manner. I had no idea what to make of community meetings. All I knew was that the doctor who wrote passes for leaving the hospital was there. So, I made damn sure I wouldn't miss one of them. The doctor's name was Dr. Pass. I think that he might have changed his name so people like me would get the hint. Be nice to Dr. Pass. So, as soon as I was cognizant of the fact that people could do jobs, and this was encouraged by Dr. Pass. Well, I volunteered for three of the jobs on the unit ASAP. I did greeting of new patients, cleanup crew in the dining room, and one other job which I cannot remember. I had so many of the patient jobs at one point that Dr. Pass joked, "At this rate, you're going to be doing all of the unit jobs in two weeks." His mannerism was relaxed, I was almost able to take the compliment in a good way. I could have, if he weren't some kind of demon. But, to survive in this world, you need to be political. So, I sat and smiled.

Eventually, holding onto what was left of my sanity and good behavior must have shown through, because I was told that I could get out of my solitary room and into a room with a roommate. It was a big move according to my nurse. I felt a bit uneasy about sharing a room with a lost soul, but I smiled and said, "I'll get my things." And so continued my journey into seeing how deep the rabbit hole went.

Chapter 3: My Beginnings

I was born December 17, 1972 in Bellevue Hospital in Manhattan. Nixon was still President. The Vietnam War was still raging, and almost fourty-six thousand American soldiers had lost their lives at that point in the war. Soon after my birth, mom wore a MIA-POW bracelet made of burnished copper and underneath she glued my baby identification tag. I was her little soldier. Mom has told me that there was a fire in Bellevue hospital the cold December night that I was born, and it was snowing outside. I was born prematurely on a night of bright fire and freezing ice in New York City. This mixture of fire and ice would color the rest of my life, not in a literal sense, but in a figurative sense. I have had many sublime moments throughout my life. I've been able to do many feats of strength and intelligence, this has been my fire. I have had many lonely days and sad things happen to me, as happens to all of us. This has been the ice that has clasped my heart for many a year.

I was born three months premature, so like all the other premature babies at Bellevue I was called a "little champ". Many children died in 1972 who were born as small as I. These days the care that a "preemie" will get is better. However, life and death is still a gamble. Sometimes I have asked myself, "Why was I in such a rush to face the world?" You know what? I can't remember. To this day, I feel many times that I am in a rush. Maybe it's because of the city in which I was born and raised, New York City. Its frenetic pace gets into your bones.

I was born to my mother Marye Harris and to a biological father whose name, to this day, I do not know. All I know about my biological father is that he worked as a lawyer. He was older than mom, and that according to my mother he tried to be a good man. I understand that he took on many social causes. Mom says they were in love and that he asked my grandmother for her hand. But, when my mother declined to convert to his faith, Judaism, he abandoned us. When he found out that my mother was pregnant with me, he made sure to tell her he never wanted to see me, and we would never get any money from him. He was the son of a rabbi, and I understand he was descended from the Cohen line. I didn't know until I was thirty-three and I was reading a book on Judaism that the Cohens trace their lineage back to the first High Priest of the Jewish people, to Aaron, the brother of Moses. On my mother's side, our lineage has been traced back to Charlemagne, the pilgrims and others of note in history. I think that if you research your genealogy back far enough, everybody is related to some historical figure because the world was much smaller back then. Mother was as Anglo-Saxon as they get with bits of German, Irish, Norwegian, French, Scottish, and possibly Spanish mixed in. My biological father's recent past was somewhere in Russia, being of Russian-Jewish descent.

For most of my young life, I hated my unseen biological father, and I would have gladly hurt him badly, given the chance. I think many kids who are abandoned by parents feel this way. I don't blame my younger self for hating him. I still think he made the wrong decision, leaving us. He missed my growing up, and I think he would have taken good care of my mother and myself. However, the world was different back in the early seventies. Society, in general, was more rigid and less forgiving than today, and as I understand it, the Jewish society, even more so. Even today, many religious Jewish men will not marry out of their faith. I would like to think that in today's more liberal society, my mother and father might have married. This is not certain, because he was orthodox Jewish. But, what was, was. Their love was not to continue, and I, the produce of a romantic encounter of theirs, live on as a living testament to what might have been.

Mom was finishing up her graduate work in the education department at Hunter while she was pregnant with me. It must have been hard for her, juggling morning sickness with the stress of classes. After she had me, it was uncertain whether I would live or die because of my premature birth. She visited me every day at the hospital. She couldn't touch me because I was in a special crib for premature babies called an incubator. Mom saw the doctors feeding me intravenously through my feet because I was too small to take in nourishment though my mouth. As mom tells it, one day, the doctors said to mom, "We are going to try Will on some liquid food. Today will determine if he will live or die." After some initial choking, I was able to ingest the liquid food, and thank God, and, thanks to my own will to live, I lived.

***

My first memory is of a taxi ride home with my Chinese stepfather Yu Jiang, mom, and a bundle of joy that would grow up to be my lifelong best friend. That bundle of joy was my younger brother Leaf. I must have been three years old. It is quite a powerful memory since I can still remember it foggily today. It was night. The taxi traveled the streets of midtown Manhattan and zipped by under the lights of the city that never sleeps. I found myself as an older brother. Mom saw to it that I'd be a good one. As far back as I can remember, I have always enjoyed being a nurturing, older brother.

My second earliest memory is of mom talking to me. I think Leaf was somewhere in the vicinity. I was very young. Mom said to me, "Will, this man (my Chinese stepfather Yu), is a good man. He is going to take care of us. I want you to treat him like your own father." I could sense great sadness her. I resolved to make her proud of me, and from that day on I made myself respect and even love my stepfather as if he were better than my own biological father who abandoned us. This man must be better, I thought. I must have been about four years old. I had broad shoulders to carry large emotional burdens, even back then. I never complained. I grinned and beared it.

My mother and stepfather tell me that, at about two years of age, I stood up in my stepfather's blue Mustang, and I pointed to a McDonald's "M" sign, and I mouthed a sound.. "mmmm". Mom took that as an early sign that I would be a precocious child. After half a year of Kindergarten, I was placed in first grade because I was deemed bright beyond my years. From being the "boy under the slide" with the cute girls in kindergarten, I became the youngest in a class of strangers. I remember the night before I went to first grade. I woke up panic-stricken that I would be going to a class full of kids I didn't know. Mom comforted me. However, as time played out, my fears would prove to be well-founded. I had social troubles for various reasons for the next few years as a youngster at Public School 59.

Even some loser teacher, when I was in sixth grade, jumped down my throat. We had just gone on a trip, and the substitute teacher we had for a day was asking some questions from a sheet of paper. I knew every answer to every question, and I was one of those annoying kids that wanted to show the teacher that I had been paying attention. The rest of the class was pretty much silent for most of the questions. So, this middle-aged, balding, short and bitter male substitute teacher says to me, in front of the class, "You think you are pretty smart. But, let me tell you something. If I gave the class an assignment, and I broke it up for them, they would know the subject better than you. They'd be better than you." This logic devastated me. I was despondent the rest of the day, and I didn't raise my hand for anything. Looking back, it is hard to believe that people like him are allowed to take care of children. I think he reacted the way he did because he recognized my intelligence and was jealous. He wanted to take me down a peg because he was a petty and bitter man.

Regardless, I loved learning, and I graduated as the valedictorian of my elementary school class. The valedictorian was decided by the "Citywide" exam, a comprehensive exam given to all sixth grade students in New York City. I scored in the top one percent in the city in reading and math when I was in sixth grade. That meant that I could supposedly read and do math at the same level as an average twelfth grader. I remember the graduation ceremony, everyone was getting their "most improved" and other type of awards with much attention and applause. Then, the award for valedictorian came up. It was a very abbreviated congratulations. It seemed to me that the teachers hurried that honor, for whatever reason. I didn't understand that this should be a pretty big deal until, later, when I looked at my award and looked up the word "Valedictorian".

I was always a good reader because mom gave special attention to my reading abilities from a very young age. To this day, she'd say that I was a "born reader". She'd play with me by putting cards around the apartment and we'd enjoy playing reading together. When I got older, we'd go to Donnell library on Fiftieth Street as a treat. I remember those days. I always loved going to the library. I remember being fascinated by Greek Mythology when I was in the fourth grade. Most people when they touch on the Greek myths really enjoy them, I think. I memorized them to the extent that, one day, on a field trip to the Metropolitan Museum, a guide asked the class if anyone knew the story of Hercules. Hercules was one of my favorite stories from the Greek Myths, so I raised my hand. The guide asked if I could tell Hercules' story to the class. So, for the next five minutes or so, I rattled off one of the versions of the death of Hercules. It was fun to share a little of what I knew with others.

However, I was not always good at math. In the third grade, I struggled with the multiplication tables. I just didn't quite get it. Poor math skills were unacceptable to my stepfather, daddy Yu. He resolved that summer to get me up to speed with my math during our family trip to Lake George. It was that summer when I learned to think mathematically. At Lake George we all stayed at a bungalow about five minutes walk from the lake. This was to be one of my favorite trips of my childhood. I remember the first day we got there, I was upset about missing the latest "Dukes of Hazzard" show. I am happy to say that I learned to live without the TV that summer. The country is a blessing for a city kid. Mixed in with the mathematical education that summer was a lot of fun playing with my brothers Leaf and Chung. We went swimming in Lake George, fishing, canoeing, and playing sports in the sun. Great times. The only thing that was unpleasant was father's math lessons. Looking back, dad's lessons were like medicine. They left a bad taste in your mouth, but they were good for you. So, we had math workbooks we worked with. I believe they are still selling the Spectrum series math workbooks. I had to do one entire page of math in the workbook every day, about thirty problems. I couldn't play or do anything fun until that was done. Leaf was made to do math as well. In the beginning, it was very hard to discipline myself. However, at the end of the summer, my math skills and ability to discipline myself were much improved. At that point it wasn't so bad, and the math usually took about an hour because I learned to work quickly. I had learned to do word problems, calculate simple and compound interest, the Pythagorean Theorem, and I learned how to find the surface area and volume of basic geometric solids that were not curved. When I got back from summer vacation, I went from being one of the worst math students to the best in my class, in grade four. In retrospect, it was really amazing how much I grew with some attention.

Chung and Leaf were cool guys to hang out with at Lake George. This was the first time I hung out with my stepbrother Chung. He let me borrow a book titled "The Silver Chair". I found the Narnia series by C.S. Lewis fascinating. I remember that the giants and the magic of the world of Narnia drew me in like nothing else that I had read before. I never really read fiction until this introduction. Before this, I only liked reading non-fiction. However, my pattern of reading would change, due to Chung's influence. The majority of books I would read for pleasure in the next years would be fiction. Leaf and I learned how to fish with Chung that summer. Our first fishing pole was a cane pole. All three of us shared it. We caught carp and sunnies with American-made, tempered steel hooks. I found Chung to be cool the first time I met him, and I still do think he's a good guy. I discovered that it's nice having an older brother.

***

I experienced a bunch of really powerful moments as a young boy. One of the most powerful was the day Leaf realized we weren't totally blood brothers. I think he was seven or eight. One day, out of the blue, I mentioned that it was too bad we weren't fully related. He was crushed. He didn't believe me at first. He couldn't wrap his head around the thought. I was told this fact when I was three or four. I helped him understand that it's ok. We're still brothers. The next day, he was positive again. A night of sleep did him good. I always tried to give Leaf strength of mind and confidence that were not given to me by my stepfather. I think I did well, because of Leaf's self-confidence, he has always been one of the popular kids in his class. I felt good about that.

When Leaf was only five, I was eight. I remember horsing around with him, as children are expected to do, pretty much all the time. I was taking him home from school, alone, without adult supervision. One day, we're horsing around on a New York City corner, and the next moment Leaf is in the street and his head is almost run over by a city bus. I grew up too fast in that split second. I resolved to keep Leaf safe, from that moment on. I'm glad I didn't kill my best friend. I don't know how I could have lived with that burden. The shame and the guilt would have been very heavy on me. Furthermore, my sister-in-law Dora couldn't have married him. His two beautiful daughters Viki and Cindy would never have been born, and the world would have been a darker place for his loss. Sometimes I ask myself when thinking about that horrible thing that almost took place, "Why was I allowed to take care of such a young child in such a big city, when I was only a child?"

In childhood I had one experience that seems of clinical interest, really, in retrospect. When I was very young I would look at a metal filing cabinet in my room, closely. I remember seeing many faces in the flecks of metal of the old cabinet: faces of demons and the lost, mostly. They were faces that were made of flecks of metal. Patterns. I have an uncanny gift for making out faces from inanimate objects. I don't know what this says about the makeup of my mind. My brother Justice, years later, gave me a test once where there were faces hidden in a picture. Supposedly, most people given this test could pick out five. You were considered excellent if you found seven. I found twelve.

Chapter 4: A Promising Young Life

Between elementary school and Junior High. I grew. I really grew. I grew roughly eight inches in four months. I was 6'2" and eleven years old at the beginning of seventh grade. I was growing out of my clothes like Abraham Lincoln did. During "Rookie Day" the older kids didn't pick on me because they thought I was one of them. And, I didn't join in picking on the younger kids. I thought it was wrong to pick on weaker kids because I was in that position in elementary school. I was placed in the "SP" classes "SP" stood for "Special Placement", because I had done well on the Citywide exams. The SP kids were the brightest of my junior high school, Wagner. I resolved to be cool in Wagner. I yearned to fit in. And, I did. I became one of the popular kids. It was a nice change of pace. I was still bright, I always got decent grades. However, the grades were not such good grades that it would be considered "uncool", and I didn't study that much. But, it was a good time. I made friends at Wagner that would last into High School. I still remember many of my Wagner friends with good feelings. By the time I finished with Wagner, I had two science Regents under my belt and one math Regents. A Regents high school diploma was the best kind of diploma you could get in New York State. A student could only earn the Regents diploma if he or she passed the Regents tests. I was on the road of academic achievement early. I took the specialized high school test in the ninth grade and I got into Stuyvesant High School with flying colors. Only the top students were allowed to attend the specialized high schools, and of the specialized high schools in New York City, Stuyvesant High School was the hardest to get into. This was a big deal to me.

Getting into Stuyvesant High School at that point in my young life was the Alpha and the Omega. It was everything. It meant I would have a good future, and it meant that I would have a successful life. I remember getting the news that I was accepted. I ran out of my homeroom and bounced off the walls of my junior high like a ball because I couldn't control my happiness. It was an amazing thing I had done. On my form of the exam I was number seventeen in all of New York City. My score was 636 out of 800, and I had beaten the number required to get into Stuy by well over one hundred points. Success!

I remember the first day at Stuyvesant was overwhelming. So many kids! I was lost in the crush of youth. The workload started immediately. We were given a lot of homework from day one. No dilly-dallying for us. I figured that I'd be a very social guy, so I didn't study much. I knew I could not afford to go to an "ivy league" school even if I got in because of lack of financial support from my family-- and time would prove that realization correct. So, I was social and enjoyed my time at Stuyvesant. I would do anything to get out of work. Such is the folly of youth.

However, despite not trying, I had talent. At Stuy when a literature teacher gave out a new book, I usually devoured it that night after class, and usually I had it finished by class time the next day. I remember one literature PhD who was teaching us at Stuy ask jokingly about a Gothic-type reading we were assigned the day before, "Has anyone finished the book I assigned to you yesterday?" I was the only one who raised their hand. She just stared at me, and shook her head. In retrospect, I don't think she believed me. I was a bit of a character in high school, and I guess I had a reputation for being a bit unruly. Looking back, I regret giving my homeroom teacher so much grief.

I was a popular and gregarious guy, in the golden period of my life. For some reason, people opened up to me. I was like everybody's older brother. I was entrusted with very personal stories from a number of people, like I was a therapist. I think I had a presence that said to people, "It's ok. I'm on your side." Also, I did not judge people.. I didn't use my strengths to pick on people. I used my strengths to support people. This came back to me big time one day.

I was hanging out in the park near Stuy when a female, Chinese friend of mine came up to me. It was one fine spring day in the park near Stuy. She asked if she could sit down. "Sure", I said. After sitting, she confessed something that made me feel glad. "Before I met you, Will", she said, "I was afraid to open up to people, to life. But because I have met you, your influence has made me open up to people, and I just wanted to thank you." I was floored, and I was happy for my friend. I didn't know what I could say, so we hugged. It was a happy moment. I knew I touched my brother Leaf in a similar way, but to have a peer who is unrelated to you, give you such words was a real honor.

I was a very physically active young man. I bicycled, ran, played basketball, played American handball, and I liked to play sports in general. One of my "things" was strength training with push ups. I remember when I was in the Boy Scouts, one of the older guys bragged about being able to do a hundred pushups in a row. I must have subconsciously put that in my mind as some kind of goal. So, when my body had matured enough to try to do strength training, I had something to shoot for. When I was sixteen, I decided that I probably wouldn't grow anymore, so why not be serious about the training now? I started with 30 push ups in a row. That made me really sore. But, after time, I was able to do 50 in a row then 60. Then 100! I did something that I called overtraining to achieve this. I would wake up in the morning and do 50 push ups, then at night, before bed, I would do another 50. I slowly increased the repetitions and number of sets until I was doing hundreds of push ups in the morning and hundreds at night. I did this for a few months, slowly getting stronger and stronger.

I recall reading a short story about a Knight of King Arthur's Round Table named Percival. He searched the backstreets of London on a dark, foggy English night to bring Jack the Ripper to justice. Percival could only see by the muted blue gaslight streetlamps and could easily be ambushed; however, he felt no fear. It was a really well-written story, I thought. Percival eventually apprehended The Ripper. So, it ended well. One of the reasons Percival was not afraid was because of his great strength. The story said that it felt as if he had a "band of steel" across his chest. At the time, I understood what that meant, because I also had a "band of steel" across mine.

Doing hundreds of push ups with no apparent goal becomes boring. So, finally, I decided that I would give myself a goal and try to do the next level up. My goal became 1,000 push-ups in a day. For a week, I mulled over if I was ready for this physical feat. Then one day, I decided to go for it. I gave myself an afternoon to accomplish this feat. My first set of push ups was of 100. I felt good after that. I rested for 2 minutes. Then, I did another set of 100. Still felt good. Rested 5 minutes. Did another set of 100. I felt good, not as good as after the first 100, but still good. I did one last set of 100. I completed it, strong. No problems yet, but I decided if I were to complete the entire 1,000 I'd need to conserve strength. The next 12 sets were sets of 50. It was really challenging, and I'd be lying if I said my last set of 50 was as well done as my first 100. But, I did it! Yes!!! It took me slightly over 2 hours to do 1,000 push ups! I was really happy and tired. For the next few days, I rested. My muscles were really sore after that exertion. Being tired is one thing, but something happened that causes me concern in retrospect. It was a sign. Whatever I was doing to my body was somehow affecting my mind. It was not only a physical sign of exercise, but somehow it was also a mental sign.

After not having done any exercises or push ups for about 3 weeks, I was walking around the corridors of Stuy during my lunch period, and out of nowhere came a desire to hurt someone. I imagined that I would just go into one of the stairwells, and knock someone down one of the stairwells. The urge was almost absolute. Almost. I decided to bring myself to the nurse's office because part of me was totally against this idea. I went to the nurse's office and told the nurse on duty what was going through my mind. She seemed startled, and said that I should go lie down. So, I did. After about thirty minutes, the urge passed. She sent me on my way soon after. This small incident shows me one thing very clearly, my powers of insight. Although I had a strong urge to smash someone's face in, and at that point in time, I definitely had the brawn to do it, some part of me knew, that at my core, I was against it. It is to that core to which I am very grateful, I knew myself at a very deep level. Self-knowledge is a helpful thing when struggling with a mental illness. Heck, it's helpful if you aren't.

***

The most powerful experience I would have at Stuy was my first girlfriend. I'll call her "Love".   Love was an older, pretty Chinese girl. We went to different high schools. I went to a high school that was very selective. She didn't. She was taking calculus. So was I. She couldn't believe that at Stuy we had 45 minutes of calculus and were ahead of her class, even though they had an hour and a half of instruction daily. I thought I was in love. She made me feel alive. We had a young romance. She liked it when I carried her up a flight of stairs with one arm. We were both paiges at the Mid-Manhattan Branch of the New York Public Library.

I remember our first romantic encounter. I had met her a few days prior. She was working on the third floor of the Mid Manhattan Branch of New York Public Library on 40th street and Fifth Avenue, and I was working on the fifth floor. We took the D train together to her neighborhood in Brighton Beach, Brooklyn. We had a nice conversation, and I felt very attracted to her on that trip. It was a cold November day. We walked down the high stairs at the D train Brighton Beach Stop. We strolled down to the boardwalk, and sat next to each other. I remember she was cold, so I lent her my Stuyvesant High School Cycopaths bicycle team jacket. We huddled together, but I was excited, so I wasn't cold. She asked me questions like, "Do you like me?" And, it was pretty obvious that she did like me. So, we hung out by the sea, listening to the seagulls and listening to the murmur of the surf. We talked and bonded.

Eventually, we started kissing. That was nice, and a new experience for me. We ended the day under the boardwalk, making out. Every time I hear the song "Under the Boardwalk" by The Drifters, I drift back to that memory, and it brings a smile to my face. We would be making out under the boardwalk almost every day until winter rolled around. We were so hot together that even on cold, wet rainy days, we'd look forward to being together, under the boardwalk. We did this, because she was scared about her mom finding out that she had a boyfriend. I respected this sentiment, and let things take their course.

I remember the first day I was invited to Love's house. It was near Ocean Avenue, a small and nondescript three level house. I remember the cats. There were at least two. The females in her family were crazy about cats, I would find out. Her cats liked me, so it seemed I was good to go. Her mom couldn't believe how tall and young I was. At the time, I was sixteen, and Love was twenty-one. When she finally told me her real age, I was so in love, I didn't care how old she was. Love had two sisters and two cousins. They seemed tight-knit, and happy. I traveled the two hour train ride each way to be with her almost every day. Eventually, I would start sleeping over at the suggestion of her mother.

Love liked my strength. For the last four months of high school I worked at an internship in a computer operations department for the department of Housing Preservation and Development, near her high school. We hung out frequently at the South Street Seaport, Chinatown, and in her neighbor-hood. Those were good times. We hung out at Brighton Beach a lot, and it was a very romantic period of my life. However, not everything was perfect. I let friends slip as people who are attached frequently do. Looking back, I do regret that many of my high school friends are no longer in my life. I had the con-viction that none of my friends studied hard and that I didn't want that characteristic to rub off anymore now that I was try-ing to be a man. To me there were three things that I wanted to take care of at that point in my life: my Love, my education, and my family.

Chapter 5: Giving it the "Old College Try": Stonybrook University

My younger brother Leaf is a gifted writer. He wrote the following poem which message I bought into when I was a younger man.

The Inequality of Life

If truth > a champagne life,
then it is easy to tell that life = beautiful
If you think that sex is a function of x,
or that (money + Harvard) = success
then you = deluded.
Life is 10% great iff
there exists a woman such that
if for every action,
there is an equal but opposite reaction.
Life is 98% great iff
1+3=42 and life is not a constant.

The body of this poem highlights the things that most people equate with success are really just false dreams. I think this way of thinking is a mark of being brought up poor but bright. We didn't get the BMW when we graduated from high school. We knew we would earn everything that would come to us. So, things of substance were prized, and material things were relatively unimportant. In college I thought there were only two things that were in my life that would endure: my love for my girlfriend and my education.

I remember the summer before I moved to the State University of New York at Stonybrook campus. I needed a job to supplement the small amount of money my parents were giving me for college. So, I went to Stonybrook to plan my next four years. I walked around the sprawling campus, analyzing it. I went to the Student Union to see what it offered. I took meticulous notes in a composition notebook. I walked around the administration building where I found the Human Resources department. It was there at Human Resources that I found that I could get a part time job as a state worker and still be a full time student. The carpenters needed three years of carpentry experience. The laborers needed a driver's license. I was seventeen, so I couldn't drive yet. On the job board my eye caught "Part Time Cleaner". There were no educational requirements. I had to be able to lift light loads. I didn't need the driver's license. It paid eight bucks per hour. Nice. I applied for the job, and I rushed back to the train station. I caught the 4:17pm train home.

Three weeks later, I got a call from Stonybrook. They scheduled an interview with me, and I was to meet the head of the janitorial department. I was so psyched! Eight dollars an hour! That was $32 per day and $160 per week. I had to get this job so I could afford to go to Stonybrook. I would do almost anything for this job. I got an interview suit, and tickets for the Long Island Railroad. On the day of the interview, the worst possible thing that could happen, happened! I was running late because of a train delay. So, I called the head janitor's office to tell them I'd be late for the interview, fearing the worst. They told me it was ok, just get there as soon as possible. So, I got myself out there, used a map to find my way to the Physical Plant, the secretary of the chief Janitor seated me, and I waited nervously.

"Come on in." I heard in front of me. I looked up, and I saw a man of medium stature with a smile on his face. I was put at ease. "I like your suit." He said. I smiled. "Thanks." I said. He sized me up pretty quickly. He could tell I'd be a good worker, and he liked my positive, can-do attitude. After talking a few minutes, he stood up and he said, "You got the job. Let's see how you do. My secretary will give you your starting date." I thanked him, and got the start date from his secretary.

The evening before I was to start work as a part time cleaner, I took the last train out of Pennsylvania Station on the Long Island Railroad. I missed a connection at Jamaica station. This was bad. I was told by the LIRR train guys how to get to Stonybrook if I would take a cab when I was out on Long Island. So, I did that. I took a train, and then I took a cab to Stonybrook campus. I arrived about 4am, and I was to start work at 9am. It was a good thing that I only had to kill five hours. I was where I had to be at 9am. The boss was pleased.

We took a pickup truck to the South P Parking lot. South P was a sprawling concrete parking lot for the commuter students at Stonybrook. There were a lot of commuter students, and it was far away from campus. It was so far away that there were buses that ran from South P to all places on campus. The day was sunny and mild. Clouds scudded across the blue sky. There was a lot of garbage on the ground, because there was a temporary amusement park there the week before. I remember there was a young Puerto Rican guy there who was telling me his marijuana stories. I just did my job. He didn't seem like a bad guy, but I didn't want anything to do with the drug thing. The day passed quickly because of the physical labor, and when we were finished cleaning the parking lot, it looked as if the amusement park were never there. Good job.

I moved into my dorm room later that day. I had the clothes

on my back and $2.50 in my pocket. I remember feeling hungry around dinner time, and I recalled there was a 7-Eleven near the campus. I walked over to the 7-Eleven with the smell of the dorm still in my nostrils. As I walked to the 7-Eleven I experienced a smell that you don't get in the city. Fresh air and a dark Long Island night. It was better than the air in Central Park. I walked into the 7-Eleven, assaulted by the bright fluorescent lights. I walked around the store. I remember the hot dogs looked good, but I didn't have enough money. So, I bought a jar of chunky Tostitos salsa. Salsa for dinner. It wasn't what I wanted, but it was dinner. I got back to my dorm room, and drank the cold salsa out of the jar. The problem was that I was still hungry. But, I couldn't eat until tomorrow until the food services opened. So, I went to sleep hungry. Thus ended my first big day at Stonybrook.

In many ways college is supposed to be a time of growth. I kept that in mind during a class called COR 101. It taught the literature of the Canon. What is the Canon? The Canon is the sum total of the great books of the Western Civilization. It was in this class that I was introduced to Homer's Odyssey, Dante's Inferno, Virgil's Aneid, Sir Thomas Moore's Utopia, and many other great works. This class started a fire in me to read the great literature of Western civilization. I remember our professor, he was a chubby, middle-aged, Caucasian, sprightly guy. He had buckets of energy. He had his PhD in history from Harvard; therefore, he was able to put these great works of literature into beautiful focus and historical context in a way a literature professor couldn't. The two years of my life at Stonybrook before my first hospitalization consisted of academic work, eating, tutoring and studying with Love, doing the janitor thing, and not really anything else.

I had so little money that I couldn't buy a Coke to enjoy during my long nights at work. However, when my classmates laughed at a small hole in a sock I was wearing to a jogging class, I bought some new socks begrudgingly because I didn't like being laughed at, not because I could afford them. By the end of sophomore year, I was in senior standing, I had taken some of the most difficult classes at the university, and I was planning to take a twenty-three credit load the next semester, heavy with advanced math, science, and English literature classes. I was a member of two honor societies: Sigma Beta and Golden Key. Life was good. Then, one day it all came undone.

Chapter 6: The Rough Ride Through Stonybrook

I met a young guy in the COR 101 class, let's say his name was Ganesh. He was Greek, and we enjoyed talking about the big issues in our young lives: girls, God, and greed. We were fast friends. I remember talking about class assignments with him and it was always interesting to hear his perspective. We disagreed frequently, but we never really fought. That was part of the friendship, the friendly disagreements.

I remember one time we were walking around campus, and we were discussing God. I was bringing up the standard negative talking points of an atheist about religion: religious people seem brainwashed, it is impossible to prove or disprove God, and oh yeah there were those little abuses on humanity called the Crusades and the Spanish Inquisition. Ganesh just looked at me. He started talking about the structure of things. He argued that if God didn't exist, how could there be any order to things? How could there be order on a micro or macro scale? I told him, there just is. I remember we had that same disagreement a few times. Sometimes, we had other people join in the debates. It was always fun trying to see things through that guy's eyes, and I think he liked to see things through mine. We generally liked grabbing meals together whenever we could. We'd just hang out and chat over Crystal Pepsi. It was always good to be with good company.

I lived in the G and H Quads for a few weeks. They were the dorms for, primarily, the underclassmen. I hated it there. One night, after I got back from work at 1am, some fools pulled the fire alarm five times. I resolved to get out. So, I put in for a move to Kelly Quad. I wanted to live with some upperclassmen because I thought they'd be more serious about their academics. The difference between the lowerclassmen and the upperclassmen turned out to be six of one was half a dozen of the other. I remember the upperclassmen jokers I lived with at Kelly Quad. They were drunk at least once per week, and they didn't seem to be too serious about anything. It was difficult to live with them, especially as they saw it their duty to mess with me from time to time. It was hard being a young, motivated student in a place filled with jokers.

I worked the Social and Behavioral Sciences building during the 11pm-3am shift, from Sunday through Thursday. I remember my first night on the job. It was hard. I was seventeen. The supervisor was a hip, short, middle-aged lady. She showed me my area, and told me what I had to do. I remember it was very dark that first night. The wind howled outside the building, and the elevators behaved as if there were ghosts using them. Imagine this: two in the morning, the doors to elevators opening and closing as if there were people using them, despite the fact nobody was in the building. That was eerie, and it was very late. So, when three am arrived, I left promptly. I didn't want to spend any more time in that building than necessary. However, I quickly became used to the grueling routine. I made a habit of going back to my dorm room as soon as possible after work, to sleep.

I took twelve credits that first semester: Physics, Calculus for engineers, COR 101 where we would read the "Canon" or great books of Western Literature, and a jogging class. Because I was only taking twelve credits, I had some free time to read things I liked. I read books about the medieval troubadours of Europe, and many other things. I joined a Karate class, and I had a relaxed semester. I remember taking books outside of the dorms and reading on the grass in the warm sun. It was so pleasant. Great days. The mild sun, the warm breeze, and the learning that was afoot were a great combination. I loved those college days.

Near the beginning of my semester, I wanted to get some people to form a study group for calculus. I didn't want to take a chance on a bad grade. So, after the first class, I handed out fliers saying, if you want to join a study group, see me. I didn't get any response, except from this one tall, statuesque redhead. She told me that she'd study anything, anytime, anywhere with me. I was shocked, because I never had such an easy time picking up a girl, especially when that was not my intention. I smiled and I talked to her a bit, I told her that I had a girlfriend and thanks but no thanks. I saw her around campus once in a while, but I didn't do anything with her. I considered myself taken because I had Love in my life. I studied almost every day at the Frank Melville Library with Love. I found it easier to concentrate in a library setting than in my dorm room. I liked the community atmosphere of studying there. I generally would be at the library when I was not at my dorm sleeping. The only other exception would be when I went to the meal halls to grab some food.

When I first moved to campus, people complaining how bad the cooking was in the meal halls. I disagreed with them silently because where I came from, Mom's tuna fish aspic was really much worse than any of the cafeteria food that we were served at Stonybrook. These people were from a different world than I was in many ways. I ate boiled turkey, without salt, nearly every day for ten years. In my house, if we didn't eat the food, we went hungry. It was much nicer to have the food at Stonybrook. It had taste, at least.

I really don't know why I did some things when I was a younger man. One time, when I met a guy that seemed to be a real fool, in the cafeteria, I played a trick. I remember Love was there as were two or three other people, who I already knew. I wasn't always a nice guy. In the conversation, he asked me what I was studying. I told him I was a neurosurgeon. He bought it hook, line and sinker even though I was only seventeen. We had a discussion on the complexities of the human brain, and at the end of the conversation, I still had him fooled. It was funny to see his expression when he thought a neurosurgeon was eating at the same table as he was. I was like a god. That wasn't nice of me, and I did meet this guy a bunch of times later. I told him the truth, eventually. But, he never made a fuss about being hoodwinked.

I did well that semester. I got an A in calculus. I got a B+ in physics. I would have gotten an A in physics but my lab reports were messy. To this day, my brother Chung characterizes my handwriting as "epileptic chicken scratch". The physics professor Dr. Lee was very nice about things. He saw that I was a hard working young man, and that I got one question correct on the final regarding fluid dynamics that nobody else had gotten right, and I did have the highest average in the class, including one perfect score. He even told me he'd like a guy like me as an intern. He may have been hinting to me, but I wasn't planning a career as a physicist. It was hard to swallow a B+ when I got such high grades on the exams for that class. But, oh well, those are the breaks! I got a B+ in COR 101, probably because of my "confused" style of essay writing. I understood and remembered the texts probably as well as anyone else there, but I never wrote well that semester. These days, I'm thinking that my confused way of writing is and always has been due to an underlying brain disorder.

The gym class I took that semester was called basic running, but you'd never know it the way the guys in the class competed. Soon after the class began, we'd run hard, forming a line, and we'd take turns leading the group. We were kind of like a peloton formation of racing bicycles, except we were runners. We all pushed each other to go faster, and there was no room for weakness to show. We'd run on and off campus. We'd do up to five miles each day. I was averaging sub seven minute miles for the five mile runs. So, I was doing ok. I kept up with the other guys. Sometimes though, I would be dropped because of stomach cramps. Running that fast that far made my stomach really knot up. It was like someone took a knife to my stomach. So, that was that. There was an Asian guy in the class, a strong runner. He was always at the gym. The group would usually sprint the last two hundred yards to the "finish line" near the gym. We did that just to keep things interesting. The Chinese guy won the sprint a good number of times. But, I had a win as well.

One time, we were running around Cedar Road, off campus,

and the guys seemed to be going a little slower than usual. So, I said to myself that I'd mess with them. I upped my pace a bit, and kept it up. They didn't latch on. So, I kept going. I dusted them. One minute turned into two, into five, then into ten minutes. I looked back over my shoulder, and surprisingly, I didn't see them. Finally, I made it to the LIRR train station, alone. I had one of those knife cramps in my stomach, a bad one. I walked for two minutes to take it easy. I was still in pain, but this was a chance to win the day's race. I jogged slowly past the train station, and kept going despite the pain, towards campus. When I was about 100 yards into the campus, I saw the other guys running hard to try to catch me, at a fierce clip. So, I upped my pace too. The Asian guy with the huge calves lead them. I was 200 yards away from the finish line when I heard his feet slapping on the pavement. I lost it, and I ran as hard as I could. After a monumental personal effort, I won the race that day, and I was in pain. It was a good pain though. One of the guys told me his perspective as to what happened. "You pulled ahead over a hill, and we thought we'd catch you soon, but you were gone. Good run, man!" The Asian guy also congratulated me. It was a great day.

After taking that class I'd run all over campus just to keep in shape. It took me three minutes to run from my job to my dorm which was probably three quarters of a mile away. I remember two situations where my younger brother Leaf came to campus, and I used the "speed". One time, he wanted to catch the 4:15 pm train back to New York City. We heard the train whistle. We were about half a mile away. It was impossible for him to catch the train if we didn't run. So, I yelled to him, "Run!" I grabbed his forty pound bag, and I ran hard. He couldn't believe how fast I ran because I got to the train way before he did, despite the weight. My brother Leaf has always been a strong guy as well. There was another time where he couldn't catch me in a small twenty by forty foot padded room. I was incredulous that in a room that small, I could evade that guy for ten minutes. Leaf ain't slow.

Love and I studied together every day. We were inseparable. We'd go to the library most days to study. Though I loved her, she was a tax on my spirit. One day I had enough. We had a rocky relationship, and I wanted out. I told her I'm dumping her. She cried, and ran out into the rain towards a construction area on campus. She was acting hysterical, and I thought she might hurt herself, the way she was acting. I thought I couldn't let her hurt herself. So, I ran after her. To make a long story short, I took her back because she said she couldn't live without me. We went back to studying together, and life continued in its imperfect manner.

That semester I did well. I got an A in Calculus, B+ in COR

101, B+ in Physics, and A in Running. I had a 3.63 average, and that qualified me for the Campus Sigma Beta Honor Society. Mom, Dad, Justice, and Leaf came to visit to celebrate with me. I remember being happy to see them. We all went out to a Chinese restaurant near campus. It was fast food, but I didn't care because it wasn't every day I could eat Chinese. My younger brother Justice was there. He threw a rock at Love, and he busted her lip. I was furious, but you can't beat on a kid that is only two. He was lucky he was so young. The punk. The celebration was over too fast, and I had to get back to work.

I had a good job as a janitor, Mom said, and so I had to hold onto it, even through the winter when nobody was around. I rented a room near campus that winter so I could keep the job. It was six miles from campus, and I commuted with a Giant brand mountain bike. The room was a small one that was in the back basement of a house near Port Jefferson. The house was small and nondescript. I paid $400 per month for rent, and it was one of the most boring and dangerous times of my life. I hated commuting to and from work late at night by bicycle. The Long Island roads are really creepy three in the morning. Did I mention it was dangerous as well? I don't know what the hell I would have done if I had gotten a flat. Yeah, there was that. I had no light to bike by most of the trip, except for the moon and stars. Luckily I could see pretty well by starlight. The only time I got a good view of my surroundings on the road was when an infrequent car would pass me. They must have thought that I was crazy being on those freezing roads in the deep of winter, that late at night. They'd be right. Looking back at that time, I wonder why mom and dad didn't just tell me to forget about the eight dollar an hour job I had because no job that pays so little is worth risking your life every day. Even the military is possibly safer, in general, because you have a team and equipment backing you up. It certainly pays more.

Maybe my parents didn't counsel me well then for the same reason they made me go to kindergarten via the Manhattan bus system alone at five years of age in the crime-ridden seventies. No, not the school bus system. That would have been too good. The public transportation system. I guess when I was younger I felt I was invulnerable. Hey, I was a big boy at five. Of course, I'd be a big man by eighteen, a real man, a scholar, and an athlete. I was able to do the twelve mile round trip to work in less than an hour most times. The bicycle was quite reliable and well built, except for one time when I was grocery shopping. I pushed down on one of the pedals, hard because I had to get across a wide highway to get to the supermarket, and the pedal broke. It was plastic. So, I guess combination of the cold, the force of the push, and maybe a defect in its manufacture caused me to tumble onto the highway. I remember distinctly that I was wearing a blue leather coat, a sweater, and a helmet. So, I tumbled to the blacktop and got up fast. While tumbling, a car going fifty miles per hour or so came within three feet of my head. Had I landed differently, I wouldn't be here telling my tale. So, like I said, I got up quickly, and I pedaled across the rest of the highway like my life depended on it, because it did.

One night, about two in the morning, at work at the Social and Behavioral Sciences Building, I was drained. I couldn't face the long bike ride home that night. I called a person in the Unitarian Universalist church congregation, near campus. I don't know exactly why I called him. But, he told me that he had good news, that I didn't have to bike home that night. He could get me a room on campus that night. I was ecstatic! He told me to go to Kelly Quad after work, in a particular residence and there would be a guy that would let me stay with him. So, after a long night of work, I biked over to the location that I was supposed to go, and I dialed the guy's number. He came out, saw I was quite wet from the precipitation that night, and motioned for me to enter.

I don't remember the guy's name. I do remember he helped me dry my wet shoes in a coin-operated dryer. He helped me dry my clothes also. I was happy for a bit. We were having some random conversation in his room, and I was in the middle of thanking him, when my eyes landed on a video he had in his room. Something about gay sailors, I think it was. I said something to the effect of, "That looks like a really fucking gay movie. Why do you have that movie?" And, I laughed. He didn't laugh. With a serious face he looked at me and said, "I'm gay." I was shocked that any decent person could be gay. This was a first for me. I was young and homophobic, but it was too late to go bike home. So I stayed. It was difficult to get to sleep that night, and I woke early after a fitful sleep. Looking back at the situation, I know that this was the first gay person I met who I considered to be a "good person". I hope that guy wherever he is can forgive the disparagement I unintentionally gave him. He didn't deserve that. He was just trying to help out a fellow traveler.

That morning, I woke up early, and I left his place quietly with my bicycle. I was quiet so I wouldn't wake him. I closed the door behind me, silently. Then, I walked down a short hallway, and out into the cold, winter air. There was snow and ice on the ground, some white, some dirty gray. I jumped on my bicycle relieved to be on my own power once again. I bicycled the six miles "home".

The most uncomfortable time I had on Long Island that

winter was the day I bicycled to an optometrist's and then to Smithtown from Port Jeff. It was a long trip in the freezing, winter rain. I didn't have money for a raincoat that would work on a bicycle, so I had fashioned one out of garbage bags. I got to the optometrist ok. But, after I got back on the bike, my makeshift raincoat was no longer functioning. I bicycled to the nearest train station. Smithtown. By the time I got to the eatery at Smithtown, I was shivering uncontrollably. The waitress was concerned. She brought me a cup of hot cocoa. After about ten minutes of the hot cocoa and the warmer air in the restaurant, I was feeling a little better. I was soaked through and cold, but I was not shivering. I went back out into the cold to catch the train back to Stonybrook, and I remember saying to myself that there was no way in hell I'd live on Long Island over the winter without a car, ever again. Now, I equated winter with suffering. Unfortunately, after this winter, I thought of winter no longer as only the season of my birth, but as the season of death.

A typical day of work as a part time cleaner on Stonybrook Campus that winter involved stripping and waxing classrooms. It takes a lot of effort to make those academic buildings look good. It's not an easy job. That winter, I laid three coats of wax in every classroom on the third floor of the Humanities building. The floors were beautiful, reflecting the winter sun, almost like glass. This was my work, and I did a good job. The students would be back soon though. And, I remember two days into the spring semester that the gleaming floors of the classrooms had lost their shine. Salt and water from boots ruins the gleam of a waxed floor quickly.

I lost touch with my Greek friend that semester. I guess it's because I didn't reach out and neither did he. I had a habit of letting good people go at that point in my life. The only people that mattered at all to me were Love and my family. I had this dream that I would save my family with my hard work. I would be able to make enough money to bring them out of their ghetto neighborhood where there was a lot of drug activity and gunshots almost every night. I dreamed that I could bring them into a safer neighborhood, where they would be happy and healthy. I had not learned yet that I first needed to take care of myself before I could take care of others. This realization came much later in my life. Back then, I was all about being good to others. I've come to realize that somewhere in the middle is the balanced life. I guess the semester I let go of my Greek friend was the semester it all started going downhill. I took a large credit load that semester which consisted of mostly math and science. I was eighteen years old pulling twenty credits.

I worked so damn hard that semester. I didn't have time for anything except eating, sleeping, studying, working, going to the bathroom, and a little "quality time" with my girlfriend. I dominated a few curves. Others, not so much. I remember, leading up to finals week, that I had three papers to write and three exams to study for in three days. I had no idea how I was going to finish that work load, but I did, and I did ok. I stayed awake three days and nights in a row, cramming for a linear algebra final. I ended that course with a C+. I wasn't going to complain about the low grade, because complaining was for the weak. I'd just have to make more A's to compensate. I got all A's and A-'s that semester except for the calculus class and the linear algebra class where I scored in the C range.

Looking back, it is quite clear that I had my first symptoms of a nervous breakdown soon after that semester. It is well known that stress can aggravate and even cause mental problems. I was under a lot of stress that semester. In retrospect, it makes sense that I had prodromal symptoms because I had the genetic propensity towards a mental problem. I was alone in one of the dining halls, during the summer break. I was broke as usual, and I saw a sandwich on the floor that nobody was paying attention to. I decided to take it. I was hungry and poor. I took it and ate it quickly. Then, I started feeling sick, and I was having stomach pains. I thought the sandwich was poisoned. I ran over to the Stonybrook University Hospital. They kept me there for observation for 2 hours, and then discharged me.

There was no poison in the sandwich. The symptoms were all in my head. But, it seemed so real! The rest of the summer passed quickly, as I took four liberal arts classes. Great. The next year was a blur, I took upper-division applied math and first year computer science classes. I did better with applied math, by getting straight A's. And, with computer science, I did ok. I did well enough to continue as a computer science major. I was planning on doing that as well. The next summer I took another four liberal arts classes. I was gearing up for my first semester of senior year after only two years of undergraduate study! I was nineteen, a senior, and loving it.

I was preparing for my fall semester to begin. The three classes I took in one summer month were still fresh in my mind, and it was a beautiful day. I walked past the gardens in front of the Library to the Administration building to check on a long time endeavor. I wanted to be financially separate from my parents because then it would be easier to pay for college, and I could have a little time for myself once in a while. This way I could sleep more than five hours per day. I was expecting good news. When I was told that nothing had changed with regards to my financial status, I was devastated because I knew I was working really hard. Also, I wasn't getting adequate financial help. I think that disappointment was the straw that broke the camel's back, or in this case it was the thing that broke my mind. The stress of money was too much. So, I had my first paranoid thought at that moment. I thought that the government believed that I was trying to steal from them. So, I wandered around the campus, going through the motions of my normal life, having many paranoid thoughts.

Soon after, I got into a car with some acquaintances of mine, and I had the "realization" that they were gangsters that were part of the government plot against me. I made them to take me to the hospital because I thought that would be a safe place. I was very lucky to have been brought to the hospital at that point in time because within a few hours I would be so psychotic I thought I was an incarnation of Jesus Christ. The first part of this book describes some of what was going through my mind during my first hospitalization. It was a living hell.

Chapter 7: Back to Bedlam

Stonybrook University Hospital

I was now sharing a room with a complete stranger. A probable lost soul. I wanted none of his infernal power to rub off on me. I wanted to stay as spiritually clean as I could. Eventually, I started sensing things that were happening, activities that were going on outside on the ward. I started going to groups. The weird thing was that every time I went into a room with what looked like a ventilation duct, I felt physical vibrations emanating out of the duct that made me very uncomfortable. The vibrations were like from a huge rock concert speaker that was muted, but you could feel its power. So, I dealt with that torture, pretty much 24/7 while I was in the hospital. It was hard to concentrate because of the physical discomfort.

Love visited me almost every day. She was my lifeline. She would sing to me, and she would comfort me. I knew I'd ask her to marry me when I got out of this hellhole. That is, I told myself, if I survive the experience. She was always so pretty and small. She gave me hope.

One time my mother and younger brother Justice visited me, my doctor told me to stay on my bed. So, I stuck there like the sheets were made of glue. My mother and Justice came in a few minutes later. Mom was like, you look like you could use some exercise. I said, "Yes, that's true." So, she indicated that we should run laps around my hospital bed. I thought to myself, that's crazy, but, we did it. A nurse came in the room, and I asked her "Do you see anything strange about running laps around a gurney?" She said, "No." So, I felt even stranger. Justice was dressed up in a red jumpsuit. He was red like the devil. And, he was quite loud. I remember giving that kid rides on my bicycle when he was smaller, and now, he was bigger and louder. I wish I could say it was good to see them. But, it wasn't. The two people that gave me comfort were my brother Leaf and my Love. Period.

Love would come and teach me songs to brighten up my day.

> Mayo t'ien ni yo ja
> Mayo Ja ni yo ni
> Mayo ni ni yo woa

this translated as

> Without sky there would be no Earth
> Without Earth there would be no you.
> Without you there would be no me.

The song was very romantic, and comforting. I remember that song to this day, and I remember the way Love made me feel. I still have dreams about her. It's hard to forget your first love sometimes. She brought me food, smiles, and hope everyday.

Speaking of poetry, brother Leaf told me later that the first time he visited me, when I talked to him, I sounded as if I were reciting poetry. I thought that was odd. Now, I feel it is a compliment. I was sick as sick could be, yet I sounded as if I were reciting poetry when talking. I think that's a nice way to be sick if you are going to do it. Leaf couldn't come visit often. He was very busy in high school pulling phenomenal grades. He had to stick to schedule. Yet somehow, he did make time for me. He's always been a good brother.

I remember a poem and picture that Love brought for me. We had deep feelings for each other still, so it would take her time to leave me. The picture and poem reflected this. I can recall the picture was of a tree and a flower. I was supposedly the tree, and she was the flower. The poem read like this:

The Tree and The Flower

The tall tree protected the little flower,
So the flower could blossom and become more luxurious
Even if the flower is picked
Her root will stay forever. Forever.

These little gestures by Love meant a lot to me. We sang "our song" together some days. We heard it on the Robin Hood Soundtrack. It was the Bryan Adams "Everything I Do" song. Basically, we hung on the "Everything I do - I do it for you" lyric. It was good to be loved during this difficult part of my life.

Weeks passed. I was allowed out of the hospital on a pass with Love. She comforted me, cooked for me, and spent quality time with me. It was really sweet how she treated me so well. Then, too quickly, I had to get back to the hospital. I had successfully been out of the hospital for my first pass, and in my gut, I knew more times would follow. Coming back to the hospital, I noticed that I felt worse. I was starting to get an inkling that something was wrong with me. On the next pass out of the hospital, I began to develop insight. I remember on one pass I was hanging out at the Student Union, and there were people wearing all different colors walking by. I remember tracking them all with my eyes and making judgments about them based on the colors they wore. If I saw someone wore red, they were of the devil. If they wore yellow, they were dangerous, and affiliated with chaos. If they wore blue or green, they were decent people, not to be feared. Then, I saw a former professor walk by, wearing fluorescent orange sneakers. I knew this man to be a good man. I had no idea what to make of the fluorescent orange. It struck me as odd. I could not comprehend what this color meant with regards to him.

After that pass, I started the three mile walk back to the hospital. The rain pattered heavily on the concrete steps of the Life Sciences building. I remember thinking "The rain is in on the conspiracy. I know it." At that moment, something clicked in my mind. Rain could not be in on any kind of conspiracy. It is rain. What can I possibly be thinking? That was my first solid bit of insight. It was good to get because I now would be able to draw on it. I could learn to think around the disease to an extent.

Chapter 8: Being Doomed to be Free

I learned that Love was cheating on me after I got out of the hospital. I was crushed. However, their fling did not last, and Love and I reconciled. We got back together, but continuing the relationship made me jaded, and twisted inside. Little did I know that my second psychotic break would strike about a year after my first. Between the two hospitalizations, I was able to almost finish my university education. I remember taking "Biology for Jocks" and a bunch of other classes. I earned high grades. I had friends. Things were going "well". I was popular with the ladies. I learned how to get through college despite having a mental illness. Years later, I wrote a "how to" mini-book on making it through college with a mental illness.

I was on ten milligrams of the antipsychotic Navane when I was let out of Stonybrook University Hospital. Over the span of a year, I was weaned down to one milligram of the drug. My psychiatrist and I hoped that one day, I could be completely medication free. Getting off the medicine turned out to be a big mistake. Within three days, I was hospitalized for the second time. This time around, it wasn't the devil worshipers that were after me. No, it was the government this time. I remembered one of my doctors during my first hospitalization was named Doctor Bush, rather like the President of the same name. My illness seemed to me to be straight out like the science fiction classic Dune by Frank Herbert. In Dune there was a very political and deep culture in which, when people acted, there were feints with feints within feints. Nothing was as it seemed, and there was always a deeper level and subtext. Such was how I thought my life was. There was always something there that I could sense, but never fully realize and understand.

My second psychiatric hospitalization was at Gracie Square hospital in New York City. It was very strange to be there because I went to Wagner Junior High School in my youth, one block away, and I played American handball fewer than five blocks from the hospital many, many times with friends. It was amazing that I was in the same place I had been almost a decade earlier once again. Yet, things were so different. I remember facing skilled and difficult opponents on the handball courts at John Jay playground. Now, the opponent was my own mind; bigger, scarier, and deadlier than any of the opponents from my youth.

One incident at Gracie Square that I recall vividly is the first time I lined up for medications. I didn't want to do it. I did not want to be dependent on pills. However, I lined up. I knew then that medicine was my best and only hope to fight off the horror and terror that was my illness. I dutifully walked up to the nurses' window to take my medication. I was handed a styrofoam cup of water and a small cup containing a few colorful pills by a middle-aged female nurse. I looked down at the cup of pills in my hand, but I could not physically open my mouth. The muscles in my jaw had locked involuntarily. I could not believe it, so I slid down the wall and sat on the floor, shocked. The nurse came out of the station. She seemed very concerned. I could not even open my mouth to talk to her and tell her what was happening. I communicated with her by grunting and nodding my head. She ascertained that I was not just being difficult and understood something was wrong. I was injected with Haldol or Thorazine. The orderlies helped me to my bed. I felt much, much better, being drugged, and at peace. As I lost consciousness, I remember, feeling no fear.

I was confined at Gracie Square for two weeks, then discharged in my mom's care. They told me that the hospitals were not a revolving door. "Do not come back unless you really need it," they said. I resolved to buckle down and not go back. I should be able to handle this with the help of the medicine, I thought. I went back out to the Long Island winter, and I took up my mop and broom once again. I had another obstacle to face now, my fellow workers. Some of my co-workers were less than kind. They started playing tricks on me. It was infuriating. Not only did I have to put up with my psychiatric condition and an unfulfilling job, I had to deal with practical jokers. They added to my already high level of stress.

About two weeks later, as I was walking to work, out of nowhere, my head pivoted on my neck of its own accord. I stared at a spot in the woods, it was a small clearing, surrounded by pine trees and filled with a patch of white snow. I looked there intently for a few seconds, and after looking intently for a few moments a thought slowly developed inside my mind "You will die here, William." It was so clear, so distinct. It was as if a voice were whispering right next to my ear, yet without uttered words. I said to myself, I cannot deal with this. Something is wrong. I checked myself back into the hospital once again. I was taken to Huntington Hospital this time. It was a nice hospital. The headboards of all the gurneys were made of carved wood, and there was a large bowl of jellybeans at the nurses' station that nobody ever touched. They raised me to forty milligrams of Navane there. On ten milligrams I felt like a zombie and even more so on forty. It was as if a veil of darkness were permanently in front of my eyes, everywhere I went. Even sunny days were shrouded in darkness. This eternal night would last for many years.

Chapter 9: Picking up the Pieces of a Shattered Life

As soon as I was able, I rushed back to Long Island to see what I could do with my professors, to save the semester's work. My biology professor gave me an A- without taking the final because I had done so well on the previous two exams. I was grateful for her generosity. My Buddhism professor made me take the final during the intersession, and my literature professor who was teaching "Hopkins and His Circle" made me jump through a lot of hoops to get a B-. But, I did it! The semester was not lost! I had 117 credits to my name. All I had to do was to finish one more class, and I was a college graduate! I remembered that an independent study in the English Literature department would be possible because of my advanced standing as an English major. I decided to do the independent study with one of my favorite American literature professors. That way, I wouldn't have to live on campus, and I could just pop in and out to finish the course. There was nothing else in my life other than that course during those four months. I worked on two ten page papers through the darkness that seemed to saturate everything. Then, I waited for my grade with baited breath. I got an A on the independent study. I was happy, and, even better, I was a college graduate!

I invited my mother and father to come to my graduation. Father said he would not come. I expected this of him. He was never supportive of me. I invited my brother Leaf next. Mom and Leaf came with me on my graduation day. I was dressed in a black robe which draped down to my heels. The ceremony was boring. But, I remember having a proud feeling of accomplishment. I had graduated in four years, despite taking off an entire year due to my psychiatric illness. It was a time for happy thoughts, I thought. I recall one of the pictures Leaf took of me on the Stonybrook platform. I was wearing a powder-blue suit that had belonged to my grandfather. There was a far away look in my eyes. My mind knew that I was happy, but the sense of that happiness was dampened by the medicine which I was taking. All of my feelings were dulled by this medication. The fact that Mom and Leaf went to witness that "becoming" of mine touched my heart. It meant a lot to me. It still does.

The day that Love and I totally let go of what we had between us happened soon after we graduated, and it was a day I will never forget. It was a cold, rainy, gray day. We were at her house for two hours. We were affectionate. She walked me back to the bus stop, in the rain. I told her that she fell short of the woman I thought she was. She cried. I cried. I forget if I said goodbye. I got on the city bus when it came. I remember looking out at the road, through the raindrops on the windshield of the bus. I remember thinking that I would remember this day for the rest of my life. I felt so sad and alone. She had been my everything for almost five years. We had gone through good times and bad times, as all couples do. I cannot say that I have ever fallen in love again as deeply as that time with her, and, to this day, she still haunts my dreams some- times. She said one thing to me that really bothered me: "You treated me better than any of my other boyfriends ever have." It killed me. I treated her better than I treated myself, I knew this. In return, she abandoned me when I needed her most. My sense of justice was broken. I was depressed.

However, we kept up the facade of a friendship until she married a guy that was supposedly my "friend" back in under- graduate studies. He knew about Love and I. When she did for him what she would not do for me, I was finally able to let go. Her marriage to my university chum ended for good whatever we had.

Chapter 10: Picking Myself up by my Bootstraps, as Best as I Could

I was living at home with my family: mom, dad, Leaf, and Justice. I walked a lot to break up the long, colorless days. I walked six to nine miles everyday. I could not seem to concentrate very well. Reading had always been one of the great joys of my life, but due to the high dose of medicine I was taking, I was not able to read much. My life revolved around seeing my psychiatrist, and treating myself to a once a day to a coffee for fifty cents at the carts near Columbia Presbyterian Hospital. I took my coffee with milk and two sugars. That was the routine. That was the highlight of my day and all I could afford. I was not informed by anyone that I that could qualify for unemployment benefits while I was waiting for my disability benefit. Those days, it took more than six months to get the disability benefits. The whole system was even slower than it is today. The only money I had for those six months was one hundred dollars that Love's mother gave to me.

I met Love's mother in the 168th street A train station. She looked at me, and gave me the money over my protests. I knew that Love's mother liked me a lot, and she was sorry to see how things were ending. But, she knew that things were at an end. I hugged her, and I walked home to sleep because the medicine made me so very weary.

So, I walked six miles per day, on average. It kept me relatively thin. I weighed about 230lbs. I wore one pair of green sweatpants for four months. I didn't have money for any other clothes. I wore the same pair of pants day in and day out. I would wash them infrequently because I did not have another pair of pants to change into. And, they had holes in them. Finally, my stepfather told my mother to "Go buy Will another pair of pants." So, I went to Macy's with mom, and we picked out a pair of inexpensive khakis. I was happy to be able to wear something less tattered than what I had been wearing for so long. The sweatpants I had been wearing had large holes in them at this point, and I could tell people thought I was homeless.

One night, I was listening to the news radio for entertainment. The voice on the radio said that former President Nixon had died. It was amazing to me that such a larger-than-life figure had died before I did. I thought that it does not matter whether you are rich, famous, poor, or powerful, death is inevitable. We all die. I knew that on an intellectual level. However, in this moment, in the dark, alone with my radio, I felt death nearby. Sirens were wailing in the distance, their red and white lights illuminating the buildings next door. I felt that it might be easier to just throw myself off the fourth story of my building. It was tempting. I knew that my life would be very hard in the future. But, I decided against it. Death is so final, and I wanted to contribute something to the world with my life. I did not end my life that night.

Soon afterwards, I started to receive Social Security disability benefits. I was using my credit card for those six months to buy the antipsychotic medicines that were keeping me out of the hospital. Nobody helped me pay for them, not my family, not anyone. Every last penny of my money I had saved from my janitorial job went to my medication. I knew at this point that I needed the Navane more than I needed food. I did what I had to do to get it. Luckily, the medicine I took was inexpensive because it had a generic form available.

I decided that I needed to get into some sort of treatment program. With the doctor I was seeing at the time, I applied to a place called the Postgraduate Center For Mental Health. I needed to do something constructive with my time. I applied for the IPRT (Intensive Rehabilitation) Program. After two months I was interviewed, and I got in! The interview for IPRT was a strange thing. Its tone seemed to me to be like a job interview. I remember the woman behind the desk who was interviewing me. She was very impressive, and she made me feel that this IPRT Program was going to be the very thing that I would need to help with all my troubles. She was a saleswoman, for sure.

The first day I went to the IPRT program I was early, as I would be frequently. I looked around the room. I was exploring my new space. I noticed one quote that I remember to this day "God gives burdens, also shoulders." Reading that, I gained some fortitude. Yes, I have it bad, I thought. But, I am free. I am not in a jail or an institution. I need to do as well as I can to live my life on my own terms. People filed slowly into the classroom on the fourth floor of the Postgraduate Center for Mental Health. I was quiet. I did not want to stick out. I wanted to observe this new community of which I was to be a part. The other people were quiet as well, with one exception. There was a young, black guy, about my age who started talking to me. He seemed friendly. We had a conversation. As we talked, I kept looking out the window at the industrial look of the buildings that surrounded us. There were plumes of steam coming from the rooftops of the nearby buildings. We were in the garment district, and the place was not pretty. Nevertheless, it was functional, and that was enough. There was an old computer in the upper right corner of the classroom, and there was a black chalkboard in the front. There were chair-desks as well, but that was it.

The social workers came into the room. There was a cute little, Romanian-looking woman, and an Irish guy. They were young. They started the group by talking about what was going on with us. It was my first experience with group therapy. It was amazing! People talked about their racing thoughts, their paranoia, their inability to do things, and I could relate! For the longest time, I thought I was the only person in the world that suffered from these problems. Now I felt less alone. I was one of many that were struggling with a difficult disease. That awareness was very valuable to me. Every handle I could get on this problem was valuable. I was one step closer to being able to battle with my problem. With a disease like schizophrenia, you can't win. You can only fight it. It is the five-hundred-pound gorilla in the room with you. All you can do is take your medication as prescribed and go to see a therapist. Those are two things that can help immensely.

Leaf was out of the house these days at MIT, pursuing his electrical engineering degree. I missed that guy. However, Chung was always dependable when I needed to talk. He always had a ready ear. I remember one dinner we had at a Mexican restaurant.

"What do you feel for?" said Chung.

"I don't know. Everything looks good. Even the free tortilla chips!" I laughed, "I've never seen green salsa! What is this stuff?"

Chung gave me an epicurean answer I'm sure. I don't recall what he said, because I'm not much of a foodie. But, I decided to get a steak burrito, and he got a burrito as well.

"Mmm. This burrito is better than Taco Bell." I said.

"How dare you compare the food here to Taco Bell? There's no comparison!" Chung laughed.

"I'm going to bring the conversation to a serious place, Chung." I said, suddenly becoming somber, "I'm kind of depressed these days. I can't concentrate well, and I'm thinking a lot of what might have been."

"Ok," said Chung.

I responded: "I couldn't finish the computer science curriculum because my coding skills were not the best. I couldn't finish an applied math curriculum because I decided to go with something I could finish easily.. English Literature. I kind of regret that decision."

In response, Chung said, "Will. You've gone through a lot. You've graduated from college in four years despite everything. You're doing well. Also, you use the word "coding" for how you program. Most people wouldn't know to say that. You're really doing well. Don't you forget that."

"Thanks." I said. I meant it. Little pep talks from Chung always got me through the hard times, and he would not say something he did not mean. So, the vote of confidence felt

63

good. We spent the rest of the night talking about "missed opportunities", reminiscing, and talking about other little details of life. It reminded me that I live for real connections, and it reminded me that I've always been able to talk to my brothers. In this, I have always been rich.

I reconnected with a friend from Stonybrook soon after. Rose. She was a little, effervescent Chinese woman. I always enjoyed talking to her in college, and I knew I wanted to look her up afterwards since we both lived in NYC. We hung out at an Italian restaurant the first time we got back together. Good times.

At the IPRT program I was attending, I learned that we were supposed to do something with our lives as part of the IPRT model. I was all for this because I had not given up my driven spirit. After some deliberation, I decided on going back to school to become a children's librarian. I felt that the life of a lawyer, teacher, or businessman would be too stressful.
How stressful could a bunch of kids at story time be?
While going to IPRT, I had a job selling T-shirts. Part of my job was working with other young people, about my age. I remember one of the girls I used to work with. Frang. She was fiery, short, busty, and pretty. One time while I was earning my keep selling the T-shirts, I was paired up with her. Rain was in the forecast, so we had to keep an eye on the sky, and we had to keep the T-shirts dry. Little did I know that I would be in for a visual treat later on, thanks to those little raindrops. We had set up for the day under a large, transparent tarp. During most days, even with heavy rain, the tarp would keep us dry. The rain started early. We stayed there because we could still sell shirts in between downpours. Frang and I chatted up a storm, ourselves, as usual. She liked to talk, and so did I. Pretty soon though, the winds started up strongly and the rain did not abate. The rain and wind got ever stronger. So, I held the tent down using my own body weight while Frang covered all the tables, so the merchandise didn't get wet. There were some powerful gusts because I couldn't hold down the tent. It flew away, and Frang and I got soaked. I smiled broadly because Fang was wearing a white T-shirt, and she was looking good in that wet T-shirt. She laughed, and she called me a pervert. I could tell she liked the attention though. We got picked up and dried off after being soaked for about an hour in the warm summer rains. We went down to Chinatown to eat some Chinese food and hang out. I was poor but social, and I preferred being social to being rich. Things didn't develop between me and Frang, sadly. She had a boyfriend. But, after they broke up, she wanted to get social with me again. I was flirting with her a bit one day, and she told me to stop it. I told her that if she wanted me to stop flirting with her, she would need to

stop talking to me. That ended that friendship. I wanted more from her than she was willing to give.

I didn't make any lasting friendships at the IPRT program. I did befriend a middle-aged Jewish guy there for awhile. He was a decent sort with a strong character despite having a serious mental illness. I really tried to be his friend, but he was careless. He didn't pay enough attention when he was at the crossing lights in the busy streets of New York, and he almost got killed multiple times this way. Well, I couldn't deal with that. I ended that friendship. There was an Irish girl at IPRT that was about ten years my senior. I thought she was a nice woman, and we always had good conversation. We kept in touch for a number of years, but later because of a faux pas on my part, we could no longer be friends. It seems that I am able to get and keep friends who are "normal" better than those who have mental illnesses for some reason.

All this time I was working on my application to Queens College library school. I used a recommendation from an applied math professor that I impressed with my upper-division probability and statistics skills. She loved talking about literature with me because I was an English Literature major in an upper division applied math class. I liked her. For some reason she didn't like Love. I never quite understood why. Maybe she saw something I didn't. Also, I used a recommendation from a writing instructor with whom I was friendly. He was a good guy. For my third letter of recommendation, I submitted a recommendation from my Romanian social worker because I couldn't get any others easily. It was on letterhead from "The Postgraduate Center West". So, I'm guessing that the people at Queens College thought this was another graduate program. Lucky for me, they didn't know or think to check that this was no academic institution. Between the walking, selling T-shirts, and IPRT, time past fast enough, and soon my six months at the IPRT program were over. About that time, mom gave me a letter from Queens College. I took the letter in the white envelope from her. I saw the "Q" on the envelope. That Q was the logo for Queens College that would dominate my life for the next three years. I read the letter. It was an acceptance letter! I was elated because I had aimed for something uncertain, and I hit the mark!

Chapter 11: The Thirst for Knowledge and Hope for the Future are Again Engaged: Graduate School at Queens College

I remember travelling to the Queens College campus for the first time from Washington Heights. I took the 1 train down to 42nd street and transferred to the 7 train where I took it from its first stop to its last: Flushing, Queens. I didn't know this, but Flushing, Queens, had the second largest Chinatown in New York City. The journey to Queens College from Washington Heights was a long one, and it did not end there. After enjoying a Chinese pastry and coffee with cream and two sugars near the subway, I queued up to take the Q17 to get to the Queens College campus.

It was amazing. Queuing up for a bus was new to me. I was not used to New Yorkers getting in line for public transportation. In Manhattan they always made a mad dash or a bumrush for the bus. This was more civil. The Q17 stopped in front of a McDonalds, a block from the Subway station. I rode it to Kissena Boulevard, a block from campus. Then, I hotfooted down Kissena Boulevard along the tree-lined campus exterior, past the Spanish-style Administration building with its earthen-colored, terracotta roof shingles, to the Rosenthal Library. The Library was the most beautiful building on campus. It was a modern structure with a clock-tower. It had an atrium on the first floor where the light flooded through the large glass windows. The floor was a deep brown terracotta, and there was a lot of steel used in the building's construction. This was to be my home away from home for three years: my focus and my determination. The library school was in the basement of the Rosenthal Library. The entire trip from Washington Heights to Flushing, Queens using public transportation took me two hours each way, each day, seven days per week, for a total of four hours of commuting per day for three years, including summers. So, over the three years I was in graduate school, I commuted a total of well over three thousand hours roundtrip to campus and back. Had I known that statistic my first day, I might have be a bit daunted.

I remember that signing up for classes at the Queens College library school was an involved process. The rest of the campus was allowed to register by scantron, and later by phone. Not us. We had to go, in person, six in the morning, and sign a sheet to give us the privilege of signing up for a class at ten in the morning. The faculty and administration said this was so people would not take classes they were not prepared to enter. It was hell getting to Queens College so early. I arrived there very late my first day, around noon. By time, there were

400 people in front of me. The GSLIS (Graduate School of Library and Information Studies) student lounge was packed, as was the hallway, and the atrium in front of the GSLIS office. I had to stay there until I was one of the last to be called, that day, about seven that evening. It was to be expected, in retrospect. Some people had come at five in the morning to be first in line. They deserved to go first.

We students used the time to socialize. I noticed that there were not many men around. The student body seemed to consist of mostly middle-aged women. I got to talking with a few people, and I got to hear what classes might be good. At that point, I knew nothing about the school. I heard rumors that a professor Surprenant was a professor never to be taken, and that professor Blake's course on cataloging was good. I was never afraid of taking a class with a difficult professor. "How hard could a library school professor be?" I wondered. I talked with some random people and had some random conversation. I must have been an interesting person to talk to. Most of the student body was dressed in "work clothes" which were a lot more formal than mine. I was dressed in a burgundy Carhartt coat, a t-shirt, jeans, and sneakers. I looked more like a construction worker than a library school student. Time passed. I was called. The registering faculty member asked me which classes I wanted to take. I told him, 700- libraries and computers, and 701- introduction to librarianship. I remember noting that I was going to take Libraries and Computers with professor Surprenant, but I thought nothing of it. I was registered, and sent on my way. My first big day was over. Now, all I had to do was survive the next three years.

I had two amazing professors the first semester at Queens College: Surprenant and Sununu. I took Introduction to Librarianship with Sununu. Sununu was a Spanish guy of medium stature. His most noticeable characteristic, to a New Yorker, was his laid-back aura. I was not too worried about this class. The first class, he went around the room asking people why they wanted to be a librarian, and he joked that the standard answer was "I like books, and I like to read." So, when he got to me, he said.. "And, you! Why do you want to be a librarian?" I had an answer prepared, and I was just going to give it and be done with the formality, when he interrupted me. "Hey I know you, you're a psychopath." I was shocked into silence. How could this man know I had any kind of mental health issues. I did not think I showed any kind of problems. He continued when I was silent. "Didn't you go to Stuyvesant High School?"

"Yes." I replied.
Sununu said, "Yes, I knew I remembered you. You're one of

the Stuyvesant Psychopaths."

Wow. I thought this guy has some kind of photographic memory, it's been years since he must have seen me only once. I said, "Yes, I was one of the presidents of the Cycopaths bike club in my senior year."

Professor Sununu said, "I was one of the super-marshals at the Queensborough Bridge one year the Stuyvesant Cycopaths helped out with the Five Borough Bike Tour. You Stuyvesant students are really bright, shouldn't you be a rocket scientist or something? Why did you want to come to library school?"

I said, "I like books. I like reading, and I like computers."

"Good enough for me.", said Sununu, not missing a beat and he continued around the room, asking people why they wanted to be a librarian.

I was taking Libraries and Computers with Surprenant, he was a tall, man with an imposing presence and a white beard. I thought the class would be easy because I considered myself good with computers. I was wrong. The class was a night-mare. The rumors were true about Surprenant. He was a very harsh grader. The word that his tests would be difficult was also true. The first test shocked me. Not only did we have to memorize all the textbook content and concepts, but also we had to memorize all the illustrations and even captions to tables to get all the answers correct. I was dumbstruck. Later, I found out that many people had the old tests. I did not have the luxury of falling back on some old test. In both classes my strategy was to stick out as little as possible and do as well as possible on the tests. This was to be a perfect strategy for me, especially in Surprenant's class. I think he liked to see how much you could learn, and then push you a bit more.

He was a professor of the old school. He lectured. You learned, period. This worked for me because I did not want to stick out at all. Things went according to plan that semester. I got a B in Introduction to Librarianship and a B- in Libraries and Computers, despite being well above average on every test. It was hard to wrap my head around that B-. I was de-spondent. At that time I was still attending the IPRT Program once in a while. I happened to be there one day talking about the B- to one of my counselors. I lamented, "How will I be able to continue if I only got a B- in my strongest subject, comput-ers?" I was disheartened and crushed. I was seriously thinking of pulling out of the program. My stepfather told me. "You're going to stay in the program, until they fail you out." That kind of unequivocal response took things out of my hands a bit, and I resolved to do as well as I could for as long as I could, no matter the outcome.

The next semester I took 701 Introduction to Cataloging with

Professor Blake and 702 Introduction to Reference with Professor Brody. Professor Blake was a big man. Very big. He must have weighed over three hundred pounds. He was jolly too. He always laughed a big laugh. He was likable. I did not do as well as I would have liked in his class because somebody stole my Anglo-American Cataloging Rules. I could not afford to replace it. However, they did not steal the supplementary ones that I had bought. Somehow, I survived that course without it. I got another B-. I felt that one was deserved. Brody was an adjunct lecturer when I took her for basic reference, GLIS 702. The class was a scavenger hunt for print reference sources. I used two libraries to find the over one hundred books and other sources for which we had to make index cards. I used the library on the Queens College Campus, the Rosenthal Library. I also used the New York Public Library's Main Branch at forty second street. Between the two libraries, and my performance on the exams, I pulled an A-. It was enough to barely keep me above the B average that was required to stay in the library school program.

It was difficult to study, because of the medicines I took. However, I was able to force myself to study, badly, about one hour each day. That was it. I was fortunate that there was a lot of what I considered "busy work" in library school up to that point. We were assigned more than ten articles to read each week, and it was a lot of reading. However, I soon noticed that many of the articles were on the same subjects and just used different wording to capture the same idea. I was on to something. I was able to read four articles and do just as well as the students that read all fifteen. I was able to separate what was important from what was not. Because I took short-cuts like this throughout my first year. I hung in there and survived. I became all about working smarter and not harder. Although I was stretched to the limit to keep up, I had to study and work seven days per week. I did not allow myself any days off because I did not want to fall behind. The hard work paid off. I had the minimum of a B average after my first full year of library school, which was necessary to stay in the program.

During this first year, I lived at home, and I lived on campus. I lived at home for the first semester, but when I got tired of the commute, I rented a room in Flushing, Queens so I could be closer to school. I was barely was able to afford it, scraping by financially. I became lonely out there all by myself. After living out in Flushing for half a year I came back home. My family was dysfunctional, but at least I could live for free, and there were people to talk to instead of walls. During the second half of my first year, I started getting some real help from the government for the first time in my life. I started getting help paying my tuition from VESID. What they gave me was a free education. They paid for my CUNY graduate credits in full. My counselor at VESID advocated for me, and got me the services due to the fact that I had almost a B average in my first semester of grad school. Bless her, and bless VESID. They really helped me when I needed it, and I will not forget their generosity.

I went to a therapist and psychiatrist to get my medication over at the Postgraduate Center during much of this time. I had therapy once per week, and I saw my psychiatrist once per month. My therapist was a woman, older than myself, with fantastic legs. She kept urging me to get a girlfriend, and we even put it as a therapeutic goal. Our therapeutic relationship was interesting, but it did not last long due to the fact that she was an intern, and she had to get on her way, eventually, as interns do. I do not really remember my psychiatrist because I only saw her only fifteen minutes per month. That is not enough to base any kind of feelings on. She did her job dispensing the medicines, and I did mine by taking them as prescribed. Soon, though, I did not wish to go back to the Postgraduate Center for counseling and therapy because I wanted to see a therapist less frequently. I thought that this would allow me to concentrate on my academics more. I switched myself to The Fifth Avenue Center For Counseling and Psychotherapy at 10 West 10th street. It was a nondescript building, with only a small plaque telling the world that this was the historic Fifth Avenue Center. Freud had visited the Fifth Avenue Center on one of his trips to America. It was also one of the settings in the Jack Nicholson movie "As Good as it Gets".

I vividly remember the intake session I had there. It was held in a cramped room in the basement of the Center. I had brought my baby brother Justice who was about five at the time. The counselor who was conducting the intake session said, "Are you sure you want your younger brother here for this interview? We will be going over some very delicate topics."'

I said, "It's ok, he has heard it all before. He'll be fine just playing with his toy cars on the rug."
"Ok.", said the counselor.
Justice played with his toy cars on the rug of this interviewing room while I recounted to the therapist the horrors and the symptoms that I had gone through during my first psychotic break. Justice paid no mind to us, and he was able to just play on the tattered rug, blissful in his childhood, while storms raged in my mind. I was happy to have the little punk in my life because I liked taking care of him. I enjoyed the role of being an older brother again.

Eventually, I had a great doctor there named Dr. Augustin and my first therapist was the best therapist I would ever have. His name was Mr. Barth. The first time I saw Mr. Barth, I was quite annoyed at having to be there because I knew that the medication was the most important thing for me at the time. So, I skipped out of session and did not come to therapy for two months. But, I began to wonder whether I should go to these therapy sessions and see what he had to offer, since the times that I did go were so positive.

I went to a full therapy session one day. From then on, I looked forward to therapy sessions with him. Mr. Barth always treated me with respect, for reasons such as my attending graduate school despite using really powerful mind-altering medicines. Also, he talked to me in the manner of a coach who wants you to win for yourself. If I did not feel good going into a therapy session, I always felt good coming out. He helped me stay focused on what was important, and it was difficult when that therapeutic relationship ended. He was like an older brother to me. I feel this is what an ideal therapeutic relationship should be. Therapy should consist of a therapist not just lending an ear to hear your woes but also inspiring you to be and do your best despite everything that is going on in your life. The therapist should be able to accept you for who you are.

Soon after my first experience of barely surviving a Surprenant class, I decided that I would stick to the idea of becoming a children's librarian. I took a class that was named "The Story and the Child". I wanted to avoid technology due to my first experience with Surprenant. I walked into the class, and chatted with a few of the female students, and, as part of the conversation, I mentioned how I cannot stand kids. I didn't know it, but the professor was in the classroom listening to us talk. She started the class by going around asking people why they wanted to be in the library media profession, and then she got to me. "And you. The child-hater. Why are you in this class?" I was dumbfounded, and I said something, but I cannot recall what. After class adjourned, I looked to be in another class immediately, for multiple reasons. The biggest reason I looked for a new class was that first negative encounter with the professor. The only class that had a seat open was a class called Online and Optical Database Searching. I joined the class expecting to be left behind.

To my surprise and delight, I learned the material very well, and I was one of the better students in the class. I was so good in the class that I began tutoring my classmates. I had one fellow student who I tutored say, on a few occasions, "Thank God for Will." That acknowledgement of my contribution to the class and my fellow students was a sweet affirmation. The professor was named Kibirige, and he had written a number of books on database searching. I preferred learning the material on my own, with the manuals, so his lectures were icing on the cake. If I learned anything from him in class, that was great, if not, so be it. I learned the Dialog databank which was a collection of over 600 of the most powerful databases in the world. In those days, we used an Internet connection protocol called telnet. It was a sub-optimal interface, but we made do. Also, I learned Lexis/Nexis which was the most powerful legal and news research tool in the world at the time. We briefly covered Wilson Web which had a bunch of databases from the respected H.W. Wilson Company.

The final for Online and Optical Database Searching was given to us by Professor Kibirige, and he predicted that before the end of the night someone would finish the exam. He was right. An hour after he gave us our five research questions, I handed in my floppy disk and printouts of the search strategies and reports. I was elated. However, I only got an A- in the class, because of a bizarre question. We were supposed to find information about chicken using contact lenses. I thought it was a joke, so I didn't take it seriously. I found the correct database to search, and my query was perfect, except for one omission. I did not Boolean OR the search for (chicken OR poultry) and that made all the difference between the A and the A-. But, I did well, and I was pleased that I finished as quickly as I did. Professor Kibirige was always complimentary to me after taking his class, and this felt good.

After that resounding success, I decided I would not let Professor Surprenant's legacy intimidate me as much as it did earlier. I decided to take Libraries and the Internet. Professor Surprenant said something during one of our lectures that struck me. He said that the point of technology is to make life better for all people, and not just the rich. I liked his point of view. The textbooks we used for Libraries and the Internet were colorful and full of pictures. They did not have very much information in them, so I decided to extract the information from the books and write them in my own words. This proved to be a very good solution. I got an A on the first test. A fellow classmate of mine, also a Stuyvesant graduate got an A-. She was good to talk to when we were not cramming our heads full of library science information. She was married and twenty years my senior. There was no romantic interest, but she was a good friend.

The medicine I took gave me a lot of akathisia, so my legs would bounce and I would rock in my seat, uncomfortably, even during classes. During every class I took, I tried to go out for a little walk during the lectures, just to ease this very unpleasant side effect of the medication. I did this also during Libraries and the Internet when I could not take the agitation anymore. One time when I came back from a little walk, Dr. Surprenant called me to his desk. The class was doing some kind of assignment. I was nervous because I wasn't working with the others. He said, "Will, I've noticed that you've been helping people in the computer lab." I did not know what to say. He continued, " This will be reflected in your final grade." I did not know what that meant. So, I played it cool and said, "Thanks." That semester, besides being a student, I was the LISTSERV administrator for the GLISNET. GLISNET was the automated email list for the entire Queens College Library School. I basically weeded the list of error-generating email addresses, and I posted announcements from the faculty. The error generating email addresses were typically email address-es that were no longer valid or had full email boxes.

One day, Dr. Surprenant, proposed that I should be in charge of adding new students to the list. Internally, I balked at the idea because it would mean a lot more work. There were more than five hundred students in the library program. I said that if I did that we would be shortchanging the student body of learning how to subscribe and unsubscribe from a LISTSERV. This was very true. This is a basic skill that every librarian should have. Professor Surprenant saw that I had a point, and thankfully the matter dropped. That semester I was busy with the Libraries and the Internet, and GLISNET. When I got my grade back from Libraries and the Internet, I was ecstatic! A+! Let me tell you, patience and manners pays off if you have a psychiatric disability or not!

At this point, I had friends in Library School. I was a so-cial guy, and I had dinner with friends in the school cafeteria almost every night. I had a friend who was a former lawyer. Pauly. He was a good guy. And, I even let him know about my mental illness. We remained friends. We were friends for more than two years during our days together in library school. We spent many a day in the Student Union talking about girls and classes. I also had a female friend who was Hindu. She was a good person, and I valued her friendship.

I remember one time I was sitting with my Hindu female friend in the library school computing lab and this guy I rec-ognized but never hung out with stood up and yelled, "Eu-reka!". We asked him what was so exciting. It turns out after two years of graduate school that he finally learned he could change the point size of the font from ten to twelve. We said something to the effect of "Isn't that interesting?" But, later we were dying from laughter. I started to call the guy "ten point type". There was another interesting character I encountered in library school. This one was a dead ringer for my ex Love. Immediately, my defenses went up. The only difference between love and this woman was this Chinese woman was fifteen years Love's senior. But, she was also a manipulator. It was very good that I put up my defenses immediately. She tried to get me to help her with various projects, and I always played dumb or just said I did not have the time. I was not about to get suckered in by this woman. There was also an Italian girl that I talked to, thin as a rail, but sweeter than honey. I used to like to talk to her, just to talk. There was one conversation we had about the Spice Girls movie that I remember.

"You saw the movie Spice World?" she said, incredulous.
"Yep." I said, smug.
"Aren't you a bit old for a movie like that?", she asked.
"I brought my younger brother to the movie. It was for him." I said.
"Really?", she queried.
"Yeah, but Baby Spice was a looka.", I retorted.

She laughed, and I thought she thought I must have been some kind of big loser. However, two weeks later my male friends that I was having dinners with told me, "You should ask her out." I thought they were just being supportive, and at the time I had just gotten a girlfriend off of Yahoo! Personals. Her name was Jenny. She was an art history student, and she was darling, tall, and a little thick. Our first meeting was in Chinatown where we had a nice dinner and chat. Later we went to South Street Seaport, where we sat and chatted some more about life, the universe, and everything, all the while we were under the lights of the Brooklyn Bridge. Actually, that is how we met. I had referenced the title of the Douglas Adams book "The Hitchhiker's Guide to Life, The Universe, and Everything" in my personal ad. She got the reference, and she got me as a boyfriend.

The second date we went on was in Central Park, we just walked around and, finally, in a secluded place in the park the following dialog occurred.
"This sure is a nice place." She said.
"Sure is." I said, "I used to play bicycle tag here."
"What's that?" she asked.
"Well, it's like the grade school game tag, except using bicycles." I said.
"Sounds a bit dangerous." she said.
"Yeah well, we were a bit foolhardy in those days." I replied. "Look I'd like to bring up something that's on my mind."
"What?" she said.

"Well, I don't want you to think I'm a bad guy. But, I'm having some thoughts now..", I said.

"I don't think you're a bad guy." she replied, nudging closer.

I took the cue and kissed her, deeply. We sat there for an hour just kissing and being with each other. It was nice. Other dates we would hang out in Central Park for no apparent reason, at night, in the middle of different grassy fields. We would talk and stargaze and kiss. At the end of the month, she invited me over to her place. I had a feeling what that would mean. I brought some protection. We talked, she cooked, and we fooled around. It was a nice time. But, I realized, I did not love her. I was sad. But, soon after our first month together I let her go. I wanted to be her friend, but she could not see me anymore. She did not see me as a friend. She wanted something more. Instead of leading her on and using her, I felt it would be better to let her go.

While all this was happening, my buddies at school were trying to hook me up with the Italian girl without me understanding completely. Finally, one of them bluntly told me, "Will, ask her out. She really likes you." So, the next time I hung out with the Italian girl we chatted about a Greek guy that was nuts about her. I laughed, and asked "Why don't you just go out with him? He seems like a good guy."

She said, "I don't like him, Will. I like you."

I said, "Yeah, I like you too. You're a good friend."

She responded, "No, I LIKE you, Like you."

"Oh!" I said. "But, I have a girlfriend.", I was still going out with Jenny at the time, and I didn't want more than one woman at a time. She seemed crushed. After that, things were not right between us. In my life, when it rains women, it pours. And, because I had broken up with Jenny, and the Italian girl was out of my life, life became quite boring.

The last semester I was taking Zyprexa which allowed me to double the amount of studies I could do per day from one hour per day to two. I decided to take an intro to Java programming class as well as the thesis class. I did very well in the Java programming class. I always finished the coding assignments quickly, and on the in-class exams, I always got perfect scores. During the first test, I was not sure about my program because I was using the wrong compiler. The instructor asked me if I had any errors in my code. I did not know, I could not find any. I scoured my program and changed nothing. Half an hour later, I told him, I could not find any errors. He compiled it, and it worked perfectly. This is an A, he told, me. He had tried to trick me into changing my program! I got an A- in the class because I did not prepare for the final. But, I did not care at that point. I learned that I had the skill to become a coder, if

I cared to. I was happy about that.

The thesis class was quite a difficult class because of the sheer volume of writing we had to do. I decided that I did not want to rely on anybody else to do the thesis. This was good, because my lawyer friend, who now had his MLS and was looking for a job in between checking for the UK Soccer scores, told me about a poor soul that was waylaid by two incompetent people. I knew the guy in passing. Ten point type and the Chinese woman that looked like Love were working with him on an annotated bibliography. He had to carry them through the class. He had about double the work to do because of this, and he could not get rid of his partners. Partners in a final project that can easily run over two hundred pages make all the difference. My project ended up having about one hundred pages, and I was happy with it.

During the last third of the semester, we were to hand in our theses for feedback from our professor. I handed in my paper early for feedback. I never got it back to be able to make corrections as we were supposed to be able to do, until the day the thesis was due and by then it was too late! Sabotage! Somebody probably had taken it out of the pile in which I had placed it and did not return it until the final day it was due, on purpose. I had been screwed royally. However, I got a B- on the paper despite it being a first draft. If I had time to make some easy edits, it would have been an A-, according to my professor. I did not care too much, because I was able to graduate anyway, even with the first draft. I was now waiting for the formal degree of the Masters of Library Science and the New York Public Library Certification. At the age of twenty eight I was a MLS, and out of grad school.

Chapter 12: Seroquel: Strength and a Brush with Death

I was stuck between a rock and a hard place after graduation. I wanted to work, but I would lose my benefits if I did. I knew the benefits were necessary. Therefore, it seemed that I could not work, unless I were able to find an ideal, low-stress job that worked for me.

My new doctor suggested a new medicine for me, Seroquel, because I wanted to slim down. I was 6'2" tall and 280 pounds at this point in time. I did not look or feel healthy. I was far from my muscular and slim 195 pound high school self. Walking up a flight of stairs winded me. Me, the same guy that could run half a mile in under two minutes. I did not like being overweight one bit. Once the doctor mentioned Seroquel could help me lose weight, I pounced at the chance. I took the Seroquel as prescribed three times per day. I took a relatively high dose when I stabilized on it: 600mg per day, the highest dose used back then being 750mg/day. I started working out because I started feeling less tired. I took it easy at first because I knew I had not worked out for a long time. After a few weeks, I noticed I was less hungry. I had more energy. I felt better. I joined the City gym down on Carmine Street. It was off the Houston train stop on the 1 train line. I started lifting weights. I used all the cardiovascular machines. I ran at least twenty minutes per day. After three months of this, I was in much better shape. I ate bean burritos at the Taco Bell on West 4th almost every day, because they were a dollar each. I could afford them.

I was more socially aware and active. My life basically consisted of traveling around the city on my mountain bike, playing sports, and working out. I remember going back to one of my old hangout spots. It was called the Cooper Club. I had taught GED math and science classes there for one year when I was going to grad school at Queens College. I went to see what was going on periodically, and I remember hanging out at the computer lab for a little bit. One time, I looked for a counselor that I was friendly with. Our conversation went something as follows:

"Hey!", I said.
"Hi there Will," said Mark.
"How's it going?", I asked.
"Pretty good. I just came back with my wife from a bicycle trip across the US. So, I feel really good."
"Wow! That must have been awesome!", I enthused.
"It was."
"You know," I said. "I'm looking for a workout buddy. Do you run?"

"Yes, I do.", he replied, "But, I'm not going to run with some jock."

I didn't know what to say.

"I'll catch you later," he said.

"Bye!", I replied.

Now people saw me as a jock. That was funny, because I did not feel like one. I definitely was not a stereotypical jock, I just was a bright guy that was in shape. It was a bittersweet moment. I was upset that he blew me off. At the same time I felt good that he associated me with being an athlete, after being overweight for so many years.

I moved to Boston for a month during my time on Seroquel. It was great, hanging out with my brother Leaf on the MIT campus. He had an old computer in his lab that I could use to just browse the web. I remember it was a 45MHz computer that handled Netscape easily. These days, we think a computer is old if it is below 1,000 MHz or 1GHz. I am under no such illusion. Our computing power is far beyond that necessary for most websites and word processing programs, which are probably the most useful programs most people use.

Leaf, Dora and I went jogging a few times. Dora was a strong little lady who would go on to marry my brother. I felt a bit threatened by her because I was in good shape, but the medicine made me shut down sometimes during workouts, and I did not want a little lady to make me look weak in front of my bro Leaf. Leaf, Dora, and I went for a seven mile run around the Charles river one day, and I stayed with Leaf and Dora pretty much the entire time. The day was a summer day that was not too hot, and the sky was clear and blue. Leaf said, "Let's pick up the pace." So we did. The trees along the river went by faster as we picked up speed. At near the fifth mile, I was in pain. But, I kept pace because I did not want Dora to beat me. It was a stupid macho thing. At about the sixth mile, Dora stopped running, and I thanked God privately. I stopped jogging after about twenty more strides, exhausted. I said, "That was a really good run!" Leaf came back to us, and we all walked together across the Harvard Bridge over the Charles River.

At the time, I was working to spread the idea that people with psychiatric diagnoses could work. I set up a website www.geocities.com/rite2work. On it, I presented my research on the demographics that showed that many people with psychiatric diagnoses wanted to work, despite the system that kept them in forced indolence and below the poverty level. I was definitely one of those people. I sent out mass mailings to Newsgroups on the Usenet, part of the Internet. I asked people to support all people's right to work. I got more than one hundred people to sign the petition, and then something very exciting happened. There was a bill introduced in the Congress which would support people with psychiatric disabilities, getting them back to work. I was ecstatic, and I started following the bill day to day as it traveled through the Congress using www. thomas.gov and the free newswires.

Something began to change in my perception of reality. I started getting moody on the Seroquel. I started getting angry for no reason. I remember scaring my mother with the force of my anger. For more than a second, that felt good. But, I noticed my rage growing and growing. It seemed to be tied to the bill that was going through Congress, which I was watching so intently. Eventually, my mood cycles would revolve around the news regarding the bill's status in the Senate. It came close to days before the end of Congress's session. The deadline came and went. I was distraught. My rage became unbearable. I thought about hanging myself off the George Washington Bridge in protest of the unfair treatment of the bill in Congress. I found a force of anger that was burning white hot inside that inexorably was being turned outwards towards the world, including my family. I was consumed by rage. I was like a bull that was seeing red all day. I was afraid of nothing and nobody. I realized that if I did not check myself into a hospital, somebody would die by my hand. I could not let that happen. Going to sleep, the night before I checked myself into the psych ward, I crossed my arms in front of my body like a mummy does. I do not know what that meant to me, but that was the most difficult night of my young life. I did not sleep. My eleven year old baby brother shared the room with me and slept only a few feet away from my bed. He was not aware of anything amiss. When morning came, I walked to the Columbia-Presbyterian Emergency Room, hoping to be seen and admitted before I did something horrible.

"Hello," said the nurse that was doing triage.

"Hi," I said. She did a standard intake. She included the psychiatric intake questions when I told her that I have paranoid schizophrenia and I would like to be admitted. She asked, "Are you paranoid?"

"No." I responded.

"Do you think people are out to get you?"

"No." I said.

"Well, I don't see how we can help you today", she started saying.

I was dismayed, "I really need to be in a psych ward", I said.

"Well, are you having thoughts of hurting yourself or others?", she said, in conclusion.

"Yes, definitely," I was relieved to answer. All of a sudden she looked startled and scared. They got me into the psych area of the ER. I was stripped down and given a hospital gown, with some big guards watching me. I was happy they were there. I could not overpower all of them, I thought.

I kept a grip on my composure. I did not want to cause any trouble, but I felt like a kettle of water that was about to let off some steam. They let me into the psych ER quickly. I lay on one of the gurneys until one of the other patients started picking on another. They were two Hispanic guys. I told the aggressor, with a flash in my eye, that if he wanted to remain unhurt, he would leave the other guy alone. The aggressor backed off quickly when he saw I was serious. And, it was relatively quiet for the rest of my time in the Psych ER. A psychiatrist came to interview me. He asked why I was in the hospital, and I let everything that was pent up, out. The hot tears ran down my face as I told the doctor how I was going to kill my family, and how I did not want it to happen. He was shocked, but he got me some tissues, and he reassured me that I was in the right place. I did not relax that much, but I did feel better about my decision.

Eventually, I was hospitalized at the, now relocated, Eye 6 unit. The unit was named Eye 6 because it was located in the Eye Institute building where they fixed all sorts of eye problems. I was there for two weeks. All the doctors referred to the burgundy bag I used for working out sessions as a "jock bag", but in a positive way. I was put on some Klonopin, and it seemed like a miracle drug, because all my anger melted away. After two weeks, I was discharged on Klonopin and Seroquel. The doctors wished me luck, as they always do. However, after about a month on the outside, the anger started to overwhelm the Klonopin. It came back in full force within a space of only two days. I was scared for myself and my family. We were upstate, and I told father that I wanted to get home as soon as possible because my anger is back. He told me to shut up, and we will leave in a day. He was very stupid to do that because I barely had a hold on my anger. So, I sat in my family's trailer for a day, by myself, doing absolutely nothing, the flames of anger burning red hot in my mind and thinking of nothing but getting out of there.

The next day, we left the Catskills, and we got back to NYC. I decided to get myself back on the Zyprexa. I went down to the Fifth Avenue Center for Counseling and Psychotherapy, and I politely asked the doctor there if I could get back on Zyprexa. I told him I would rather feel like a zombie than become a killer. He looked at me, and soon after that, I had my prescription. That man saved my life. I took the Zyprexa as soon as I could. About two weeks later, I was much less angry. After about two months, I hardly felt anything. I was back to the emotional numbness that I knew would envelop me for years. No joy. No sorrow. No highs nor lows. I was safe to continue living as well as I could, without emotion. Truth be told, it is better to feel nothing than a consuming rage. Holding on to anger is like grasping a hot coal with the intent of throwing it at someone else; you are the one who gets burned.

Chapter 13: New York City Voices: Finding that I Still Can Work

I was let out of the hospital, and I had nothing to do. I could not go to work, because I was afraid that my medical benefits would be taken away. I also could not exercise because the Zyprexa made me a marshmallow. I decided I would go back to the IPRT day treatment program. However, old habits die hard. I submitted an article to New York City Voices, the mental health newspaper, about a new antipsychotic that I was going to try. Here is the article:

Catching up with Zeldox
Published in the fall 2000 edition of NYC Voices
William R. Jiang, MLS
Being a paranoid schizophrenic, I am waiting with baited breath along with many others for any news about the next anticipated "blockbuster" drug Zeldox from Pfizer.

Some history: On July 19, 2000 the FDA advisory panel approved Zeldox nine to one. I thought it would be a matter of weeks until it was approved. I find out now, months later, that the FDA doesn't move that fast. Pfizer received an "approvable" letter with steps that it should take for an FDA approval on September 8, 2000. As of this writing, Pfizer and the FDA are in labeling discussions right now. Pfizer wants a good label without a "black box" warning of cardiac risk that the FDA may impose.

To do a little background research for this article, my first stop was the FDA's website at www.fda.gov and clicked the "search" box on the main page. It allowed me to search their whole site for any news about Zeldox. I got seven hits. One of the seven hits was the actual document in PDF format that Pfizer submitted to the FDA for renewal. After reading this document I was impressed with what a good drug Zeldox seemed to be. So, it seemed that Zeldox would be a good move for me. My next question was, "When will Zeldox come out?" So I checked Dow Jones Interactive at the Science and Industry Business Library at 34th and Madison in Manhattan. From that vast databank of business knowledge I learned that Zeldox is being held up by labeling issues and would probably be hitting the markets early in 2001. It shouldn't be too long before I could get my hands on some Zeldox.

To keep the picture balanced I thought I'd do some more research on the Web. I came up with some interesting statistics. "... patients in the ziprasidone group were less likely to relapse after 52 weeks as compared with those in the placebo group. Approximately 70 percent of placebo users relapsed, only between 30-40 percent of the ziprasidone [Zeldox] users did (source: www.pslgroup.com/dg/131696.htm). I couldn't believe that. That sounded like a pretty high relapse rate to me. Here's another interesting statistic: with good management the current relapse rate is about 9% (source: www.mcg.edu/Resources/MH/sourcebk/sect2.html). I don't know where these people are getting their statistics, but 9% versus 30% seemed to be a relatively large discrepancy. I guess even though Pfizer is saying Zeldox is a good drug it's best to be cautiously optimistic. I had some second thoughts, but I think with my psychiatrist's approval I'd be one of the first in line!

Soon after, in early 2000, full of boredom, while I was waiting to apply to the IPRT Program at The Postgraduate Center, once again. I got a call.

"Hello. May I speak to William Jiang?", said the voice on the other end of the line.

"Speaking", I said.

"My name is Dan Frey, and I'm calling about your article 'Catching up with Zeldox. I think it is very good, and I'd like to publish it."

I was ecstatic. I had never been published before, and this was a great compliment, in my eyes.

"Also, I'm looking for volunteers.", said Mr. Frey. "Would you be interested in a position at City Voices?"

"Yes! Definitely!" I said.

Dan Frey gave me the information I needed to start working. I began working at City Voices three days per week. I learned quickly that New York City Voices, or "City Voices", as we called it, was a program of the Mental Health Association of NYC. We shared office space with them. Mr. Frey became known as "Danny" to me. He was a very motivated, charismatic individual whom I greatly esteemed both because he gave me a break, and we were very similar in many respects. For example he went to Bronx Science, the great rival to my High School, Stuyvesant. Second, we both were into role-playing games as youths. We both had played Dungeons and Dragons. We both shared Jewish blood. We both loved the soundtrack to Conan the Barbarian. It was almost as if I had found a younger clone of me, albeit higher functioning because he was on less medicine. He was a good guy.

Danny introduced me to the legacy that he was continuing, of the now deceased mental health advocate, Ken Steele. Ken was a figure that was larger-than-life. When I went to my first City Voices steering committee meeting, I was amazed at the outpouring of support for Danny's continuance of City Voices from high-powered people. There was a mainframe operator that ran the City Voices website, a lawyer that dealt with large real estate deals, and a bunch of others. The meeting was packed. Their loyalty to the memory of this man, Ken Steele, was impressive. I became dedicated to the cause of helping others with mental illnesses by using stories of recovery and the newspaper as a medium to disseminate useful, timely information to tens of thousands of people who could use a hand.

The next important article that Danny asked me to write was about Saint Dymphna the patron saint of the mentally ill. He asked me to write it because Ken was Catholic, and we were celebrating his beliefs and his life in that particular issue of City Voices. The following are that article and a few others:

Saint Dymphna: Patron Saint Of The Mentally Ill
Published in the spring 2001 edition of NYC Voices
William R. Jiang, MLS

Saint Dymphna in popular legend is the daughter of a pagan Celtic chieftain named Damon. Dymphna was Christian. It is thought she died around 650 A.D. She ran from home with her confessor, St. Gerebernus and two companions after the death of her mother so she could escape the incestuous interest of her father.

There are two scenarios to explain why Dymphna's father had this incestuous interest for his daughter. Both scenarios show the king went insane after the death of his wife. The first scenario was that after searching through the whole kingdom for a woman as good and beautiful as his late wife, he realized that this daughter was the only one who could take his late wife's place. The second scenario was that he tried to marry his daughter because he thought it was the best thing to do for political stability in his lands.

Saint Gerebernus, Dymphna, and their two companions fled to Antwerp, and built an oratory at Gheel, near Amsterdam, where they lived as hermits. Dymphna's father found them in a number of months, and his men put the priest and two companions to death, whereas Dymphna was beheaded by her own father because she refused to return with him to his lands. When the bodies of Dymphna and Gerebernus were discovered at Gheel in the 13th century, cures for epileptics, the insane, and the possessed were reported many in number. Saint Dymphna is the patron saint of epileptics and those suffering from mental illness. Her relics are reported to cure insanity and epilepsy. When the old church of Saint Dymphna in Gheel was destroyed by fire in 1489 it was replaced by a new church, which was consecrated in 1532.

Under Dymphna's patronage, the inhabitants of Gheel have been known for the care they have given to those with mental illness. By the close of the 13th century, an infirmary was built. Today the town possesses a first class sanitarium, one of the largest and most efficient colonies for the mentally ill in the world. Gheel was one of the first to start a program where the insane inhabitants lead normal and useful lives in the homes of farmers or local residents. The strength of Dymphna's cult is evidenced by this compassionate work of the people of Gheel for the mentally ill at a time when they were universally neglected or treated with hostility.

Saint Dymphna's feast day is May 15.

In between writing articles for City Voices and volunteering with odd jobs at the City Voice office, Danny, myself, and a bunch of others would go out for lunch at fast food places. We would probably have preferred the food at other places; however, we simply did not have the money. People living on disability need to be as miserly as possible with their money, and no food is as cheap and filling as a McDonald's hamburger. We would all go and have animated discussions about many things. However, we always came back to talking about how we could contribute to the Newspaper's mission. I liked that about Danny. He stayed focused and on point.

Pretty soon, I was publishing my personal opinions and story of recovery. I wanted to share with the world the fact that one could get better from a mental disorder, be intelligent, and be a worthwhile person. I wrote the following articles in this vein of thought:

The Importance Of Medication Compliance
Published in the fall 2001 edition of NYC Voices
William R. Jiang, MLS

I was diagnosed with paranoid schizophrenia when I was first hospitalized late in 1992. At the age of 19 I was put on a low dose of the antipsychotic Navane -- 10mg. I couldn't stand being on the medicine because of the stigma of having to be dependent on anti-psychotics, so my psychiatrist and I worked together to taper me down to 1mg of Navane a day and then finally 0mg of Navane a day. Not surprisingly, after I got off the Navane I started to become psychotic. I thought I was a new incarnation of the Buddha because in part I was taking a Buddhism class and in part because I felt a "third eye" of electricity in the center of my forehead. Needless to say, three days later I was an inpatient in a psych ER near my University because I thought that the Feds were after me, and soon after I was on 40mg of Navane and zombified.

I have never been able to get back to those low doses of medication. To dream of getting on those low doses of medication is all I can do these days. What not to do is get off the medication totally after you have a breakdown, because if you do chances are you will have a relapse. Every relapse I've had has brought me down a peg in level of functioning. For example, after my first relapse I was able to read all day, but after my second relapse it was no longer possible to do that. Before and after my first relapse, I was a social person. After my second relapse I lost my social skills and was not able to carry on a conversation as I used to.

These days all I can do is wait and wait for better medications. I keep my eyes and ears peeled for news about new anti-psychotic medicines and wait for the "magic" one that will work wonders for me. Had I just stayed on a low dose of my old Navane, I would never have had to play this waiting game. My advice to those who have just had a psychotic break: STAY ON YOUR MEDS. Keep seeing your psychiatrist. Two out of three people will need to anyway, and do you really want to take the chance of deteriorating? This is not to say you can't lower your meds, but if you stay on a low dose of medication it is a lot safer than if you don't take any meds at all.

Even with staying on meds, the monthly relapse rates are estimated to be 3.5 percent per month. That rate of relapse rises to 11.0 percent per month for patients who have discontinued their medication. In plain English this means patients are three times more likely to relapse if they don't take their meds.

Good luck, stay well. Remember, mental health is the most important gift for a person with mental illness.

The Sick Me vs. The Well Me
Published in the fall 2001 edition of NYC Voices
William R. Jiang, MLS

I have had schizophrenic symptoms since 1992, for almost ten years now. In the time after I contracted the disease, I have somehow gotten my undergraduate degree in English and a graduate degree in Library Science. Along the way I've had to learn to reconcile the sick versus well me. One of the biggest helping hands I've received in my life is this tool of knowing somehow when I'm sick and when I'm well. The degrees are cool too.

When I am well, life is easy. I don't have to have patience

with disordered thinking, or depression. When I'm sick; however, it is a totally different story. Sometimes living day to day is a chore when you are a mentally ill person. Situations that a "healthy" person would easily deal with become insurmountable. When they happen to me and I am sick, I hope for them to just go away as soon as possible. This approach to life requires more patience than I ever had to muster when I was well.

How did I get my college degrees? Slowly. I paced myself. I went to school half-time for my Masters degree, and had to deal with many sick thoughts. How do I recognize sick thoughts versus well thoughts? That's a good question, because some people don't ever realize they are sick even when it is obvious to everyone around them. Insight, for me, is hard to come about when I am ill because the illness can be more real than reality. Kind of like a bad trip. I've never used hallucinogens, so I'm guessing that is how it must be.

How do I learn to trust people when I'm slightly psychotic? I can trust people when I am only slightly psychotic. If I were deep in psychosis, there would be no way I could do this. I juxtapose my present with my past, and I notice something aberrant about my thoughts. A friend calls them 'signposts.' When I'm being too negative or too positive I notice it, and it is dangerous. If I'm too negative, I'm usually very tired. The quick fix? Go to sleep. Feeling too good means I'll be going down the wrong road soon, so I pop a 5mg pill of Navane and I stop the euphoria. If I'm feeling paranoid and in class, I reach inside, take some medicine that my psychiatrist has graciously prescribed, and say this too will pass, and it always did, eventually. Usually, paranoia would hit me in social situations when I was finishing up my degrees, and also at night. For me, physical fatigue can bring on sick thoughts. Realizing this, and pacing myself through school really paid off.

Another trick I use for dealing with my schizophrenia in school is reality testing through others. If I'm having sensory hallucinations, then I ask people if what I'm experiencing is real. A frequent question I had and still have at night is, "Do you smell smoke?" The trick is to believe the answer you get. It's hard to trust others when you are psychotic, but if you know for an objective fact that sane people can offer insight, it helps.

In conclusion, if you are going for schooling and have a mental illness, my pearl of wisdom would be to pace yourself. You can do it. I'm mentally ill and I did. I'm living proof. I've seen intelligent people with mental illness fail in advanced studies just because they didn't pace themselves. Go half time. If in doubt, take it nice and slow. It might be frustrating at times,

but if you want it badly enough you can do it!
Op-ed: Do Neuroleptics Hinder Recovery?
Published in the spring 2002 edition of NYC Voices
William R. Jiang, MLS

I subscribed to a newsgroup alt.support.schizophrenia, and one of the serious topics of discussion was "Do antipsychotic drugs hinder our recovery from schizophrenia?" There was an article published in USA Today, March 4, 2002 titled "Mind drugs may hinder recovery" by Robert Whitaker that was part of the discussion. In the article Mr. Whitaker noted that in developing countries people with schizophrenia don't have access to medication; however, they got better! He went on to say that John Forbes Nash of recent fame from A Beautiful Mind stopped taking neuroleptic medication in 1970, and he had been getting better ever since.

Adding to this recent flurry of thinking about how neuroleptic medications are bad for people diagnosed with schizophrenia, I found an article at boston.com titled "Group stirs debate over schizophrenia" by Ellen Barry, March 3, 2002. Basically the article showed a group of people who were told that they would probably be on antipsychotic medications for the rest of their lives to treat their psychosis; however, they went into complete remission, medicine-free. These lucky people that went into complete remission work for a group called the National Empowerment Center. The article stated: "At their Lawrence nonprofit, the National Empowerment Center, they have been spreading a controversial gospel, telling mentally ill people and their families that the psychiatric establishment is lying to them about their condition."

So, what do I think about all these antipsychiatry viewpoints? I remember a statistic from the National Alliance for the Mentally Ill (NAMI) website about schizophrenia: approximately 1/3 get better, 1/3 remain the same, and 1/3 get worse ten years after their first psychotic break. I believe from personal experience that the earlier you catch the schizophrenia with medication, the lower the dose you need to take, in general. What do I think of Robert Whitaker postulating that "Mind drugs may hinder recovery?" One, I think it is a dangerous case to be made. Two, I think it is a misleading argument. Because you don't see people sick with schizophrenia in developing countries, doesn't mean that they get better. I'd like him to check his facts a little more closely so he could cite statistics about the rate of remission of schizophrenia in developing countries, and I'm sure that it would look very much like our country's statistics except it would look more like: 1/3 got better, 1/3 are still chained to things so they won't hurt themselves, and 1/3 died (at least).

What do I think about the National Empowerment Center's message that the psychiatric establishment is lying about the necessity of treatment? I think it is ridiculous and dangerous. There is a large movement on the Internet that tries to tell people that psychiatrists are lying to their patients, and it's best to think for yourselves whether or not you need medication. There are six groups I found on the Internet that espouse that position. Two are named the Antipsychiatry Coalition, and the Lunatics Liberation Front. Doctors have known for a long time that mental illnesses can go into remission all by themselves, but only for the lucky few. Mental health consumers who go along with the antipsychiatry movement will probably learn for themselves the hard way that their doctors are really there to help. I talked to my therapist about this topic in session, and he said that he couldn't believe anyone who was educated in the field would take these antipsychiatry topics seriously. I hope as few mental health consumers as possible take antipsychiatry seriously.

After a while of working with City Voices, I was given the task of being the advertising manager. I brought in over $6,000 for the 10th anniversary issue, and I averaged over $2,000 in revenue per issue. I would like to think I did well in this position because of my customer service attitude with follow-up, and general likableness. I did so well in that position, that I persuaded Danny to give me the duty of maintaining the City Voices Website. It had not been updated for over a year at one point, and I wanted to put that on my resume. I worked on the website to update it, for free. I was to get four hundred per issue to update it. I was happy with my jobs with City Voices. Danny was a good boss, and I felt like I was an integral member of a team that was doing something important. I even brought in a $15,000 grant from Eli Lilly due to a letter I wrote, on behalf of Dan Frey and City Voices.

Here is a snapshot at the reader demographics of City Voices in 2003:

City Voices Reader Demographics as of May 3, 2003
William R. Jiang, MLS

As a general preface to the presentation of the online City Voices Reader Demographic I'd like to let you, our readers, know what is happening in general with the website. Our readers are from 64 countries around the world at this point, not just New York City. Most of our readers come to us via Google! We are projecting near 200,000 hits for this year. We are getting our message of empowerment out to people that need a positive message all around the world! We are currently looking for advertisers online, but space is limited. For information of how to advertise with us e-mail me at kd3qc@yahoo.com Our reader demographics survey has been up for 3 months and to date we have gotten 62 respondents. For those who chose to answer our questionnaire, thank you for your time! There are 4 basic areas that we queried. Mental Health Status, Gender, Age, and Diagnosis.

To the heart of the matter. Most of City Voices readers are mental health consumers, the second largest group of readers are the family members of someone with a mental illness, and lastly are the mental health professionals. We are just about evenly read by males and females with a slightly male bias. Most of our readers were between 22 and 30 years of age, people aged between 31-40, 41-50, and 51-60 had equal showing among our readers, and the group that seemed to read us online least was the up to 21 years of age group. As for the diagnoses of our readers, the largest single group had a diagnosis of schizophrenia. There were as many people on our site as family members/ friends as people diagnosed with schizophrenia. The next largest group of readers were those with depression, then bipolar disorder, and our least represented groups of readers are those with schizoaffective and "other" mental conditions.

Under me the presence of City Voices on the web went from about 5,000 clicks per year to over 600,000 per year. It took me 4 days working part time to produce each issue of City Voices. It sometimes went up before the print edition was finished with layout. I was proud of that efficiency. However, I thought that the production of the website could be automated somehow. I talked to my brother Leaf, and he suggested I learn the programming language Perl. It took me about one month to learn Perl. I wrote a program that took specially formatted text files as input, and it would output Web Pages that I could string together for a finished product. I was able to generate a thirty-five page website in under four hours. Plus, I added the functionality of ads on the web pages, so we generated money using the website selling advertising as well. The website went from being a nice thing that got the word out to more people and generating leads for stories and new talent to a source of income for the paper.

The City Voices story would run on for years.

Chapter 14   A Librarian is Made: Kingsborough Community College

For me, work is a very important part of recovery. Without work, I feel I have less dignity and self-respect. The following articles represent different stages of my getting back into the workforce.

Work is Important in My Recovery
Having a job is a source of pride and accomplishment
Published in the fall 2002 edition of NYC Voices
William R. Jiang, MLS

In all my years of receiving care for my paranoid schizophrenia the best therapy I've had is the work I have done. I've done and continue to receive individual cognitive-behavioral therapy with a good therapist. I've done the group therapy thing at an IPRT (Intensive Psychiatric Rehabilitation Therapy) which gave me the perspective that I'm not the only one out there that is suffering with this horrible disease. The idea that I'm one of a group really helped. I continue to take a combination of typical and atypical antipsychotics that keep me in the land of the sane.

There is something self-validating about a job, and it gives me a sense of dignity that I don't have when I'm out of a job. I worked my way through college. It was kind of the "Good Will Hunting" thing. I was an honors student, and I was also a janitor. Thoughts of working on differential equations and calculating non-linear regression models would be in my head while I would be wet mopping bathrooms.

That was my job situation then. Many years lapsed before I could work again. Currently, I am working part-time as a computer instructor over at the Post Graduate Center West. Everyone over there is great, and they make it a pleasure to go to work each day. I teach MS Word, MS Excel, MS PowerPoint, MS Access, the Windows 95 and 98 operating systems and general computer knowledge. We just went for a field trip to Comp USA last week. That was fun. I'd love to teach the Internet and all its subtle complexities to my students, but currently we do not have the funds to wire our classroom. Hopefully, in the future we will be able to do that because I think the greatest single computer skill today is how to use a Web browser to harness the World Wide Web.

Thanks to the experimental New York Works program, which is a joint program between the New York State Department of Labor (DOL) and the Social Security Administration (SSA), I can now work! New York Works is what has enabled me to work part-time and keep my all-important benefits. Before I joined New York Works I was deathly afraid of going to work because I didn't want to lose my benefits that allow me to see a psychiatrist and get my medicine. I couldn't afford the risk. The people in New York Works have been very supportive of my career goals. If anybody in the upper echelons of the DOL or SSA is reading this article, I'd like for you to know that your efforts are really appreciated and make a difference!

The Ticket to Work Incentives Act that was passed by Clinton on December 17, 1999 has spawned the realization of a Medic-aid buy-in that was approved in Albany this year. This Medicaid buy-in will give many more people with psychiatric disabilities the ability to reap the benefits of work: monetary and other-wise. My winter holiday wish for all of my fellow mental health care recipients is the following: may 2003 be a year of health, and may it be a year of new beginnings with regards to your long, put-off career ambitions!

***

While I was teaching computers at Postgraduate, I was at-tending a class in Medical Reference at New York University. I wanted to get as much reference experience under my belt as well as I could. Because I was in the New York Works program, I was emboldened to go for a job in the field I have a masters, library science. I saw a part-time job listing from Kingsborough Community College as an adjunct lecturer. I ap-plied. I was happy to be called back three months later for an interview.

I arrived at the Kingsborough library two hours early. I did not want to take a chance and be late to such an important interview. I walked to the reference desk that was staffed by a pleasant, older, white-haired librarian, and she told me to wait in the library until I was called. I was impressed with the beauty of the campus. It was one of the most attractive cam-puses I have ever seen. Kingsborough Community College was situated right next to the water in Southeast Brooklyn. The grounds were so beautifully kept. I thought, CUNY knew what it was doing here.

I waited patiently, listening to my walkman to pass the time, before the interview started. Two hours later, the librarian I had talked to, whom later I would know as Jeanne, came and got me. We had a pleasant conversation as she led me upstairs to the Chief Librarian's office on the top floor of the library. The view from the ground was gorgeous, but the view from the Chief Librarian's office was absolutely breathtaking. You could see over the blue water, the white surf, and the beautifully-kept campus. That particular day was crisp and clear with a few clouds scudding across the blue sky. Gorgeous. What was to happen next was to be a rite of passage.

I was led past the administrative assistant, into a boardroom where I saw six people sitting. I was shocked when I realized they were all waiting for me. They asked difficult questions of me during the interview. The interview lasted thirty minutes. Had I known a boardroom full of people that were going to grill me for the position, I would have been much more apprehensive and probably would have been psyched out by the pressure. They asked me what I was doing now? I told them that after donating two years of my life to a non-profit organization, City Voices, I am now ready to go into the library career for which I had trained. Because I was there, I was going to make the best impression I could. As a final note, I mentioned how beautiful the campus was, and I was whisked away by Jeanne. Two months later, I got a call from Jeanne. She offered me a part time adjunct lecturer position at Kingsborough's Robert J. Kibbee Library. I was ecstatic, and I accepted.

I had a good time working the busy reference desk at Kingsborough. Sometimes, I would answer more than twenty questions per hour. There were times when it was really slow. The students came in waves. No matter what, I manned that desk and did my best. About a month into the job that, the Head of Reference, Jeanne, took me aside and told me, that I was doing a good job, and that I "think" like a librarian. I was very happy to hear that from her. It meant a lot because she knew what she was talking about, and it made me feel good about the job I was doing for the college.

The only problem with the job at Kingsborough was that there were a total of four hours commuting each day that I worked there. It was really, really hard to survive the stress that came from that commute. Because I worked eight hour days, I was putting in twelve hours straight, and when one is taking an antipsychotic, it becomes more difficult to put in so many hours. One is inclined to sleep more the higher your dose of medicine, and while I was not on a very high dose, I felt sleepy all the time. After one year of working at Kingsborough, I decided to move on. I looked for a job closer to home.

Chapter 15 Career Combined with Helping Others in my Shoes: New York State Psychiatric Institute

Following my work at Kingsborough Community College, there was a gap in my employment. I guess I should have been looking for a job while at Kingsborough, but I did not. I was still Webmaster for New York City Voices part-time. Roughly two months after I stopped working at Kingsborough, I saw an article that was to go up on the City Voices Website for the next issue. This article was about a specialized library at New York State Psychiatric Institute that dealt with educating and providing insight to people with mental disorders. I was intrigued. This was exactly the kind of work is I did with City Voices, except I'd be a librarian. I called the number that was included in the article, and I talked to a social worker that was manning the library. I asked him if they had a librarian. He said that they have people staffing the library, but they did not have anybody with the Masters of Library Science. My heart jumped. I asked who I could talk to apply to be the Patient Library's Librarian. He gave me the number of the head of Social Work, Helle Thorning. I called her, and she asked me to fax my resume and cover letter with letters of recommendations. I was happy to do so. I touched up my resume, and I wrote a brief, well crafted cover letter. I contacted my former colleagues at Kingsborough, and they were happy to give glowing recommendations. Everything was in order. I sent my resume, cover letter, and recommendations via fax, and I waited.

About a month later, I was invited to interview at Psychiatric Institute, which I would come to know as PI. I prepared myself for the interview by buying a power tie that was metallic blue decorated with white binary code. I thought it looked cool and conventional enough. I went to PI and waited for Helle in the Social Work office at 8:30am. Helle walked in, and she was a tall, thin, middle aged Caucasian woman. She had a pleasant face and demeanor with lively eyes. She grinned at me, and asked me to follow her. I did. And, she told me I would be interviewing with her and the head of Occupational and Recreational Therapy, Matt Gold. We waited for him in a room designated for the patients' families on the fifth floor. There was classic artwork and photographs on the wall. I felt pretty good about my chances of landing this job.

Helle and I made some small talk, and a little later Matt Gold entered the room. Matt is a big man in a short man's body. That is the best way I can describe him. He was middle aged and Caucasian with an intelligent, ready smile and knowing eyes. Helle and Matt interviewed me for about twenty minutes. I was confident in my Library Science skills, and I knew my former colleagues at Kingsborough would back me up. They escorted me out of the building after the interview. I thanked them, and I was on my way. They said it would take some time before they could get back to me, and that it would be moderately difficult to get the position because it did not exist yet. One month passed, and I had not heard from them. I called Matt and Helle to let them know I was still interested in the position, and asked them if I was still a candidate? Helle seemed pleased I called. Matt told me to keep on top of him, and yes, I was still a candidate. Four months passed. Matt gave me a call, he said I should come visit Helle 8:30am Monday. I had the job.

The first thing I did after I took over the librarianship at PI was design a website for the patient library. It did not yet have a nice website. I coded one over the weekend. It looked reasonably professional. Then, looked into if my brother Leaf could program my library a Web-based book catalog. It turned out that that would not happen. There was not enough money in the budget. So, I searched the web, and I found a company called Librarycom. They had OPACs, Web-based library catalogs, you could use for a dollar a day. I liked the price. I proceeded to supervise the cataloging of the five hundred plus volume book collection. It took about a month to complete the job. However, after it was done, my library had a web presence with a specialized book collection that could be searched from anywhere in the world.

While I was doing the web design and planning, I kept the library open to all comers. I found that the best educational outlets for psychoeducational materials was the NIMH (National Institute of Mental Health) and NARSAD (National Alliance on Research of Schizophrenia and Depression, now Brain and Behavior Research Foundation). I ordered many pamphlets from these sources to distribute to those who wished to learn about mental illnesses. I distributed City Voices around the Institution as a service to our patients. I brought a book cart onto the inpatient units three times per week. I brought books in English and Spanish as well as psychoeducational materials. Matt and Helle were great to work with. They were always available for advice or direction when needed. I presented what I was doing at the Psychoeducation Committee meeting every month, where we had the head of social work, head of occupational and recreational therapy, head of nursing, and other important figures in the hospital community show up to meetings. In the beginning it was a bit intimidating presenting my library in front of these high-profile people, but I took it in stride, and now, I have good feelings towards them. We are a team that is there to help the patients and their families with their psychoeducational needs.

Everything was going smoothly. Unexpectedly, my book catalog was unavailable for six months because a check was being held up by the business office. So, I decided to program my own book catalog using the web languages PHP and MySQL. After studying the PHP for a month and getting the handle of PHP MyAdmin on my personal web server. I was able to do just that. I had a volunteer enter the book data into a MS Access database, and when the data entry was done, I exported the data into a semicolon-delimited text format, and finally I uploaded it to my server, and it worked! I took the annotated video collection database and made it searchable by keyword and put it up on the web. Finally, I developed, and I continue to develop a list of very useful links that are helpful to those with mental illness, and those who care for and about them. Everything was translated into Spanish. Now, the website is a useful resource in and of itself, separate from the physical collection. It was at this point I decided to write another article for City Voices expressing my feelings towards my job and the people I was working with.

The Patient and Family Library in Washington Heights: Helping consumers as their librarian is very rewarding
Published in the spring 2007 edition of NYC Voices
William R. Jiang, MLS

I am working full-time as the librarian for the New York State Psychiatric Institute' Patient and Family Library, putting my Masters of Library Science degree to good use. I'm doing well for someone in his mid thirties who was diagnosed with paranoid schizophrenia as a teen. I credit a lot of my recovery to the fact that I work closely with my psychiatrists, and I keep a close watch on my symptoms. That way, if I feel I need to be hospitalized, I just do it. If I need to adjust my meds, I do it while letting my psychiatrist know. She usually agrees with my decisions, and I follow her guidance. We've got a team effort going.

At the Patient and Family Library, we focus on "psychoeducation" of people who are dealing with a mental illness. Psycho-education is a form of mental health treatment that includes elements of illness-education and group psychotherapy. I appreciate the care that I get more because I can now see the mental health professional side of things more clearly, and I'm committed to my ongoing recovery.

Psychoeducational materials in our library include books, pamphlets, videos, periodicals, and Internet resources. Our target customers are the psychiatric patients, family members, or people who care for others who have mental illnesses. The library is especially useful for patients who recently had their "first break" of mental illness and are still orienting themselves to the realities of having serious mental disorders. The social work interns reach out to these patients with videos from the library's collection to lead groups that spark insight and understanding. Making it out of the hospital and back into the community is aided by the insight that the patients get from library materials.

Insight is the single most important factor that has helped me to deal with my illness. Fifty percent of people with schizophrenia do not realize that there is anything wrong. I encourage people to get the medical and social treatments they need to lead their lives to the fullest.

The Patient and Family Library website has links of value to New Yorkers with mental health issues. They can get free education, legal help, vocational guidance and much more. The website is http://nyspi.org/Kolb/nyspi_pf_library/spanish_index.html or call (212) 543-6713 for more information.

***

Early in my career at Psychiatric Institute, Matt told me I could participate in a Spanish class offered by Education and Training. I have had the pleasure of learning Spanish at PI for about three years now with a great instructor named Carmen Banton. I've really flourished under her instruction, and I feel fortunate to have had the chance to become bilingual with her patient, kind help. She inspired me to take formal instruction in Spanish at City College. I'm now at the terminus of the intermediate level of Spanish. I can speak almost as well as I write, and I take every chance I can to practice speaking with people in Washington Heights. The Spanish class has also been a social opportunity for me.

I can say that learning Spanish has broadened my mind, and it helps me to aid people in my hospital who may not be able to get help easily in English. I met a medical researcher in Carmen's Spanish class that I consider one of my best buddies, Christoph. He's a very tall German scientist. I like that I can really "look up" to this man. He's a young, superstar researcher here at PI, and I'm happy to say he's just got his own lab. I helped him pick out his first computer. We go out for lunch frequently, and I'm proud to call this man my friend.

Another man that I consider a friend here is named Jack. He works with the Social Work department, and he sees to it that things go smoothly there. He's a levelheaded, Puerto Rican fellow who is a few years older than I am. I've known him since I have started here at PI, and our conversations range from the latest YouTube video, to what we did on the weekends, to politics and more. Once in a while I practice my Spanish with Jack, but usually we talk in English. He's good to know.

Another person I socialize with at PI is the Research library's librarian, David. I helped him design the main web page to the most important library at the institute and the second most important psychiatric research library in the world. The web page I made for him is still live. We grab lunch frequently. We talk about playing basketball, politics, library science, and programming and computers. David is very knowledgeable about medical librarianship in general, and he knows the structure of psychiatric information like nobody else I have ever met.

There are quite a number of people on the 4 South unit with whom I am friendly: Chuck, Marion, Eddie, Anna, and Mark. We take lunch together, and I enjoy their company. What can I say, with all these friendly people, it's a pleasure to visit their unit and work with them. I've met many good people here at PI. They make my life richer, and I'm gratified that I can be part of a team with all these people who are working hard, trying to make life better for people with psychiatric issues. When one is a patient, one frequently feels that the professionals don't care. At PI, I have found that this is not the case with the vast majority I've worked with. Most workers at PI, at the end of the day, seem to be very caring individuals whose career ambition seems to be doing the best job they can by their clients.

At the current time, I'm helping to teach conversational Spanish at PI with my teacher and mentor Carmen. I am also working with the Inwood Clinic director Dr. Dragatsi on a Spanish-language psychoeducational video about Schizophrenia. I have worked directly with MTV to get their True Life: I have Schizophrenia and other DVDs for our patient education program, run by social work. I think MTV did a great job on the video, and I thanked them for their philanthropic generosity, providing the DVDs at no cost for our patients.

The initiative I am most proud of leading at NYSPI was a Work Incentives awareness program in NYC. Despite the WIPA (Work Incentives Planning and Assistance) programs in New York City and across the nation, few people know how people with mental illnesses can go back to work and keep their benefits. When I asked directors of a few hundred mental health facilities in NYC if they had heard of the WIPA programs, most responded that they had not. So, I felt it was good that I took it upon myself to call all of the facilities in NYC to let them know how their patients could go back to work. Also, I created a pro-bono website for the WIPA programs in NYC that gives the information about how to contact WIPA in the five boroughs and beyond. I wrote about this important project in NYC Voices:

Work is Now Possible Thanks to WIPA: Rejoining the Workforce
Published in the spring 2008 edition of NYC Voices
William R. Jiang, MLS

Once I was diagnosed with paranoid schizophrenia in 1992, it was ten years before I was able to join the workforce again. I did not want to lose my medical benefits because of work. What allowed me to go back to work was a work incentives program like WIPA. The groundwork for the WIPA (Work Incentive Planning and Assistance) programs was laid with bipartisan support during the Clinton Administration. The legislation I am referring to is called

The Ticket to Work and Work Incentives Improvement Act of 1999.

I now work as a professional librarian at the NYS Psychiatric Institute's Patient and Family Library (http://nyspi.org/Kolb/nyspi_pf_library/index.html). I am reaching out to many of NYC mental health facilities via telephone, NAMI NYC Metro, and City Voices to spread the word that it is possible for us to get a good job.

The WIPA work incentives programs serve as an intermediary between Social Security and the worker, allowing the mental health consumer to work. One of the most exciting programs that the WIPA can help with is the Medicaid Buy-In. With this program, in New York State, the worker can buy Medicaid and have a gross income as high as $53,028 for an individual and $71,028 for a couple. There are other great work incentives for workers. You can contact the WIPA offices for more information.

I worked with Goodwill, Research Foundation for Mental Hygiene (RFMH), and City University of New York (The John F. Kennedy, Jr. Institute), to put up a "one-stop-shopping" website that makes it easy for people to learn about the WIPA Programs in New York's five boroughs. The website is hosted at http://www.kd3qc.com/nyc_wipa. Though this site specifically highlights WIPA in New York City, it can lead people all over the United States to their respective WIPA Programs.

For those without internet access, the following numbers can help you contact a WIPA office: Brooklyn WIPA, call: 718- 246-7855, Queens WIPA call: 718-786-2594, Manhattan and Staten Island WIPA call: (212) 385-3030 x 3139, and for Bronx WIPA call: (212) 652-2030.

I've interacted with some amazing people at PI. I had heard that we had Nobel Laureate Dr. Eric Kandel in the medical complex. I first heard him speak in educational videos I was annotating for the library. The videos were in the Healthy Minds series by Dr. Jeff Borenstein and NARSAD which were originally aired on channel 21 here in New York City. Dr. Kandel contributed to three of the videos which came out in 2006 in the Healthy Minds series: Healthy Minds: The Depression of Mike Wallace, Healthy Minds: Depression Part 2, and Healthy Minds: Alzheimer's Disease. So, I knew what he looked like, and I saw him around the institute regularly. One day, I was in an elevator with him, and I told him that we have videos that feature interviews with him and that he's like a rockstar in the patient library. I made him laugh at that. That made me feel good, because laughter is a real human connection.

***

I worked at PI for about three years when I had an important, unexpected visitor. Dr. Lieberman, the director of PI and Columbia Psychiatry among other superlative titles, came to visit me in my library one clear, spring day. I had shaken his hand at an event, and I had seen him around the Institute a few times. I got the impression that he was a soft-spoken gentleman that knew how to handle himself. When he came to visit me at my library I was impressed by his height. He was about my size, but slim. Dr. Lieberman is a middle aged, Caucasian man who has an air of authority and decision. He has authored many articles about mental illness. He brought two other people with him, the head of security for the Institute and one other lady that I know on sight. I reacted with surprise at his showing up at the library unannounced. He said that he likes to keep people on their toes. I was happy to give him a tour of the physical library: the book collection, the periodical section, the pamphlets, the computer and av room, and the video collection. He asked me if we had a film called "Living With Schizophrenia". I said, "I believe so. It sounds familiar." And I went to the video collection and promptly pulled out the video. He seemed satisfied with everything, and he left as abruptly as he came.

The second trial by fire I experienced at PI was when Dr. Lieberman and the Commissioner for the State of New York's Office of Mental Health, Dr. Michael Hogan, came to visit my library. I was told days in advance that these two powerhouses might visit my library. Laurie was the one who told me. She works with many major programs at the Institute, but I know her from the Psychoeducation committee. She was to be one of the point people for Dr. Hogan's visit. Laurie said earlier the day he came to PI that he was planning to come to my library but his itinerary was uncertain as he was pressed for time. The uncertainty gave me stress.

At the planned time he was supposed to come to the library, at noon, he did not. I thought I was off the hot seat. However, Laurie told me that they would try to get him here to my library anyway. It turned out that a little after 2pm Laurie came walking briskly into the library saying, "They're right behind me." She had a bit of pressure in her voice. Dr. Lieberman and Dr. Hogan strode into the room. I was in a state of shock. "Hello, Dr. Lieberman. Hello, Dr. Hogan." I managed to get out of my mouth. I showed Dr. Hogan around the library, like I had for Dr. Lieberman about a month earlier. Dr. Hogan is at least 6'4", and he made an imposing figure, although I'm sure this was not his intention.

I talked about our involvement with the NAMI Walk in 2007 and our Community Events that mix movies with psychoeducational content and an expert panel discussion. He seemed to know about everything I mentioned already. I was impressed. I mentioned the fact that a researcher that deals with cognitive remediation would soon be here. He seemed to be interested in learning more about what we were doing regarding cognitive remediation for people with schizophrenia. I decided to ask him if he had seen an article that struck me as interesting. The article was titled: A meta-analysis of cognitive remediation in schizophrenia." in December 2007's American Journal of Psychiatry. I thought it would be an important article to talk about when discussing the subject. The article showed a modest improvement among people with schizophrenia when this type of therapy was used. Commissioner Hogan indicated he had seen the article. I was happy to discuss the article briefly. After what seemed a fleeting minute, both Dr. Lieberman and Commissioner Hogan left. Apparently, Commissioner Hogan needed to get back to Albany. Matt winked at me and said, "Good job!" I sure felt better after hearing that from Matt. It put me more at ease. And, I was happy to see that I still had a job at the next performance evaluation. I took that to mean that I was doing something right.

When I was an undergraduate I wrote a paper on the book Siddhartha by Hermann Hesse. One of the questions I wrote about was this: how would the Buddha be in modern day life? What job would he be doing? I wrote that, instead of ferrying people back and forth as he did in Siddhartha, he would probably be working as a toll collector on the George Washington Bridge. He would help people cross the river to enlightenment in a different way because it is a different age. As a strange coincidence, my job has a beautiful view of this Bridge, the Hudson River, and the Palisades. Sometimes, when the library is a bit slow I look out at the Bridge, and I think, by helping people learn about their mental illnesses, I am contributing to their self-realization. It is an interesting coincidence that I ended up with the view of the bridge and that I am help-ing people reach out of themselves to something that can be elusive but very precious- reaching for their health. I wish all those who have picked up this book and read it, health and happiness, as I wish it for everybody who walks in through the door to my library.

Epilogue

I did not write much about my four brothers in this short book: James, Chung, Leaf, and Justice. This is because I'd need a book to talk about all the good times I've had with these guys. All throughout my life, they have been a welcome presence. I can truthfully say that my brothers have been the best friends I have had in my lifetime. I have tried to be there for them as they have been there for me. Chung, no matter how hopeless I was feeling, was there for me when I was despondent. He had a lot of influence in my picking up bicycling and reading. Leaf and I did two centuries, one-hundred mile bicycle rides, when we were younger. We loved to go fast on our out-of-tune bikes. This unconditional love for bicycling was Chung's influence. We also read much science fiction and fantasy literature such as the Dune Series by Frank Herbert, the Eternal Champion series by Michael Moorcock, the Myth Series by Asprin, the Incarnations of Immortality series by Piers Anthony, the Xanth series also by Mr. Anthony, the Hitchhikers Guide series by Douglas Adams and many more books because of Chung's influence. Also role playing was fun. I read and memorized more than ten think tomes just to learn to play the Advanced Dungeons and Dragons game.

Leaf has been a best friend and more. I wish the family he has started with his wife Dora much health and happiness. Their two ragamuffins Vicki and Cindy are the cutest!. I know my brother will do his best to take care of them all. It has been my honor to see my younger brother Justice grow from a baby to a strong, intelligent, sensible young man who is almost out of his teenage years. He makes me proud. My older sister Ching and her two kids Jessie and Jodie are definitely part of my psyche, as is her deceased husband David, who lives on in our hearts. David was very good to me, even though we were not blood-related. I hope he is in a better place, and he can watch with pride how Ching and his two young flowers, his daughters, bloom. The days I played basketball with David, on the sunny courts of Manhattan, are something I will not forget. While I am on the subject of sports, I must mention that playing American handball on the courts of Manhattan were some of the best times of my life. I introduced Leaf and Justice to the sport. Both have been better than I. Both have been worse. The thing that mattered was the quality time we all spent together, forging the bonds of brotherhood. I would not trade the times I have spent with these guys for the world.

I miss my friends from high school now. I let them go between high school and college because I thought they would be a bad influence on me academically. That may have been true, but they may have kept me more in balance, had I kept in touch. They were good guys, and though I have not seen many of them in over eighteen years, they are in my thoughts from time to time. I wish all of them the best.

They say that your friends are your fortune. At this point in my life, I feel rich. I have friends at work and outside of work. The friends at work make the day go by faster. They are good people, and I am proud to work with them in serving our clients, the patients. The friends I have out of the hospital are a boon on the days I have free. My friends online are good to hang out with when I am relaxing at home. I am never alone, and I like it that way.

What lies ahead? Nobody knows the future. The only thing that is certain is change. Our society in some ways is a society of progress, at least in the sciences. The medicines, therapies, and knowledge of the schizophrenia that has plagued me for sixteen years is becoming more advanced by the day.

Looking back, I think I and my treatment team made mistakes, but maybe I can help some people from making those same mistakes. Once diagnosed with schizophrenia I never should have gotten off the antipsychotic medicines, because I think I would have been better off long term. It may not seem that I am more disabled than after my first episode from reading my book and seeing some of my accomplishments. However, the truth is that before I was taken off the antipsychotics, I was much more able to read large quantities of information and concentrate. Even on medicines before my second break, I was able to read both Sir Gawain and the Green Knight and Sun Tzu's The Art of War in only a day each. Now either book would take more than a week to finish. I sorely miss my prior level of cognitive strength.

The director of New York State Psychiatric institute, Dr. Lieberman, reinforces this view in an experience he had when treating a young man with schizophrenia. Although I would have my psychotic break much later, this story is very relevant to the idea that people with schizophrenia should stay on their medicines. The following transcript of the acceptance speech for the Lieber prize was given by Dr. Lieberman in 2006. It appears in my book courtesy of NARSAD:

"I'd like to tell you a little story about how I happened to get into this field. It begins with an experience as a resident, in the late 1970s, treating patients with mental illness. It was a particularly motivating experience that I always vividly recall.

I was treating a young man in his early 20s. He was going to an Ivy League college, with his life fully in front of him. Then he experienced an episode of psychosis, which we diagnosed as schizophrenia. He was treated and had a full recovery, with complete symptom remission. But when he tried to go back to school, not wanting to lose the semester, he found he could not function cognitively as well as he had before. Plus, the side effects of even the low dose of haloperidol he was taking were problematic. He stopped taking his medication, relapsed and was treated again. He recovered, but again stopped taking his medicine, and again relapsed. he was re-hospitalized, and this time when he was treated, he did not fully recover. He got better with medication, but he still had symptoms, and he was never able to attain the same degree of functional capability and cognitive capacity he had previously shown.

I was being supervised in the care of this patient, and my supervisor would tell me: 'A lot of patients don't understand the illness, and they have to learn the hard way. It's good he had these relapses because it will make him understand quicker the importance of staying on his medication.

At that time, there was an assumption that you could experience these recurrent psychotic episodes, be treated and be restored as if nothing had happened. The reality is that's not true. The sine qua non of schizophrenia, which (Emil) Kraepelin (the discoverer of schizophrenia and bipolar disorder) identified 100 years ago, is the deterioration associated with the illness... [The deterioration] is not something that occurs inexorably, but it is something that potentially could be prevented through therapeutic intervention." (Lieberman, Jeffrey A. "The Lieber Prize for Outstanding Achievement in Schizophrenia Research". NARSAD Research Newsletter. Vol 18, Issue 3, Fall 2006. p4-5.

In this speech by Dr. Lieberman it shows that attitudes and knowledge regarding the treatment of schizophrenia have changed much since the seventies. It shows that the young man who Dr. Lieberman was treating would have done better had he stayed on his medicines, just as would have been true for me.

Appendix: Making It Through College With A Mental Illness

Introduction

Hello, and welcome to my book! My name is Will and I'm going to walk you through the steps necessary to graduate from college despite having a mental illness because I've been there and done that. Tall order? Not as tall as I am. I overcame that hurdle twice in my life.

The first time I was hospitalized was at Stonybrook University out in Suffolk, Long Island, where I was attending classes as English major. A psychotic break is something I wouldn't wish on anyone. I wandered about the mental ward thinking I was a saint capable of absolving sins from people by my just being near them, just like that guy from the movie Amadeus where he ends up in an asylum saying that he absolves the people around him after he confesses to the priest about killing Wolfgang Amadeus Mozart. The ironic thing is that I am not a religious person at all when I am completely sane. Amazingly, I graduated from Stonybrook University in four years with a BA despite having two major hospitalizations for my paranoid schizophrenia. Maybe if I had taken a little more time to relax and exercise during my days at Stony Brook I would have stayed sane.

Next, I went to Queens College for my graduate degree and completed that program in three years with a masters in library science. The Queens College Library Science program is a one-and-one half year program, but I knew I had to pace myself, so it took me a bit longer. Initially, I thought I'd become a children's librarian; however, it became apparent that the electronic aspect of information would become my demesnes. I had no idea how much technology would be involved in the libraries of today when I enrolled. The technology was good to me, and because I had an affinity for the electronic medium I thrived at Queens College. Because I paced myself, and I took my time, I didn't have a hospitalization during my stay at Queens College. That was good because I hate having psychotic breaks.

If you are grappling with mental illness and want to go to college, or you know someone who has a mental illness that wants to go to college, or possibly you are a caretaker of people with mental illness that want to go to college. I have designed this book with the steps necessary to succeed in college despite having a mental illness.

Chapter i: Preparing and Financing an Education

The first question any student needs to address before they choose their first class is "What do I want out of this experience?" Maybe you are good at math. Maybe writing is your passion. Maybe you see computers in your future. Maybe, maybe, maybe. Nobody knows you better than you. Guidance counselors are helpful to an extent, but if you think about how little time they can give to you, the less you'd be likely to keep their word as final. Your school's guidance counselors are obligated to take care of the entire school. You only need to take care of yourself.

Know thyself. You're going to see that phrase a lot during your studies. Who said it first? Socrates. Even before the year zero he had it correct. Some things don't really change much over the years. The best bet to succeed in college is to know your strengths and weaknesses. In college, you should exploit your strengths, and you should try to compensate for your weaknesses.

However, say you are an ace math student. This doesn't mean you take a full schedule of only math courses! That would be ridiculous! On the contrary, college is an academic adventure where each college has a core curriculum that is meant to expose college students to other ways of thinking than they are accustomed to. College is a growth experience that is meant to round you out.

Say you are weak with math. You are so weak that you need remedial training. This means that you must compensate for this weakness by filling that math requirement before you go for the classes that really interest you. The same is for students that score lackluster scores in the writing department. Math and English are the two most basic courses that are needed for a successful college education because if you are not up to a certain level, they won't graduate you.

However, if public speaking makes you symptomatic or you are not comfortable in crowds, then you need to respect these things and try not to do them, at least initially. Odds are that you will need to take a speech class and be in a lecture hall filled with fellow students. You just have to know how to survive in these situations and overcome your fears. These are all things you need to figure out before you sign up for your first class.

Where do you look to find information on schools? The World Wide Web is a good place to start. Also your local library will have books on the subject.

Where on the Web should one start looking for schools?

Yahoo! is a great place to start. Yahoo! at www.yahoo.com is more than a search engine powered by Google. It is also a hierarchically organized directory. This means there is an order to the entries, and it can be used as a reference library because it is organized by subject. It only takes a few minutes to get to the information you would need, if you had a clear idea of what you were looking for.

Also I'd recommend www.petersons.com because they are the people that make the print version of the most important print source for locating information about colleges and universities. All you need to do is go to Amazon.com and use keyword Petersons, or if you don't want to buy it, go to your local library and ask where the Petersons guide is. The librarian would be more than happy to help you. That is, unless, you live in a town with a library with only four reference books and no Internet connection! Then, your best bet is going to a decent-sized bookstore, and buying the book off the shelf. The Peterson's guide tells you many useful things, such as, the number of students in the school, the professor to student ratio, the average SAT score needed to get in. And a whole bunch of other useful things.

The necessary evil that is FAFSA is a regrettable paper-pushing experience for first time students. The good thing is that now you have a choice of picking up a paper FAFSA at your college financial aid office, and doing the FAFSA in pencil on paper. You can mail it in, or you can go to the Internet at www.fafsa.ed.gov/ and fill out the online form. If you are intimidated by computers, just know that the online option to file for financial aid is there when you grow a bit less scared of the computers.

Getting the required information and filling out the FAFSA is one of the most difficult things you will need to do to get into college. It can be very intimidating. If you can, get someone who has done one before to help you out, and don't be shy about contacting the financial aid office with any questions you may have. They may be surly and a bit disagreeable; however, they do provide invaluable assistance with all things financial. Special news about getting grant monies for school if you are certifiably disabled: you only need to sign up for 6 credits (half-time) to receive financial aid! For many years if you went to college and wanted to get grant money to help you go to college, you had to carry at least 12 credits to be full-time and eligible for financial aid! Talk to your financial aid counselor to take advantage of this great opportunity!

TAP and Pell grants are available for undergraduates who are looking to further their education. TAP and Pell grants are based on financial need. Therefore, it behooves the person seeking the grants to look as poor as possible to get the most financial aid. Don't misrepresent yourself, because they do check up on you and your family's tax forms to make sure that you aren't lying through your teeth. If you are over 21, living independently, and you are going for an undergraduate degree, you should get more than a kid that is 18 and living with their parents because the government figures the eighteen year old's parents to foot some of the bill. Also, if you are applying for financial aid, one thing to keep in mind is that you will have to sign up for selective service if you are above 18 and are male. It's the government's way of making sure there are capable people to draft in case of a large war. It's a pretty sneaky way to draft people into the armed forces though, if you ask me. However, if you are disabled, then you should have nothing to worry about because when they try to draft you, all you need to do is prove you are not fit to serve. The armed forces doesn't want people with schizophrenia armed to the teeth, and in stressful situations where they might fire on friends. It just makes sense.

Loans! This was a real big question for me. I tried to avoid using loans through most of my undergraduate years; however, I realized that I needed the loans in my graduate years. Looking back at it all, I think that student loans are a very good deal. This is why: 1) you don't start paying the interest until you get out of school, which is saving you money, 2) the interest rates are very low, 3) you have a lot of time to pay them back, and 4) loan money helps the student lead a more comfortable life while attending school, and the more comfortable a student, the better they can concentrate on their studies and getting it done the right way. The Perkins loan has a lower interest rate than the Stafford loan; however, it is more difficult to get. To get a Perkins loan you must have a very low income. Almost everybody can get a Stafford loan though. Both of these loans are very good to get because of their low interest rates and reasonable pay-back times.

Chapter 2: Your First Day of Class

Your first day of class. It's a time to be proud that you are in a collegiate environment, and it is also time to see how things work. All of your study up till now has lead to this moment, and it probably is the biggest day for you, up until your graduation from college. You should be well groomed, your first day of class. I don't mean come to school in an Armani suit, but make sure you look clean, and not dressed in rags. I knew one mentally ill student that looked mentally ill, just from his hygiene and dress. You do not want to set yourself apart from the rest of the class the way this young man did. It is in your best interest to "fit in" with the normals on the first day of class because you'll be more apt to make friends, and just feel that you don't stick out like a sore thumb, so you'll be able to concentrate on the "college experience" and academics.

What should you bring with yourself the first day of class? The essentials don't change much from undergraduate work to graduate work. You'll need a notebook, backpack, pens, and a folder to keep handouts. Also, you should bring a credit card for purchasing books that will be on your syllabi. The lines at the college bookstore are generally horrendous the first few weeks of class, but it is a necessary thing for a student to do if they want to keep up with the class. The only other option is to fall behind in terms of assignments, which is something you don't want to do in you first weeks of class because then you will be behind the eight ball (in terms of grades right from the get-go.)

The syllabi! Chances are you might have had one or two high school teachers hand out a syllabus; however, in college every class has a syllabus for you to understand what the "rules" are for each class. You may not get it at your first class, but you'll get it soon enough. On the syllabus, your responsibilities for the class and the calculation of your grade will be apparent. Chances are the books that are necessary for your class will be there. Finally, the outline of what the course is going to cover will be made plain in each syllabus.

One thing I learned as an undergraduate is: "Never trust a professor." That doesn't mean be totally paranoid about the professor not telling you the truth. It does mean that you should be on your toes to react to potential changes in the structure of the class, requirements for tests, and what will be covered on tests. The syllabus is not something written in stone. It is a general guideline for how the course will be run, and if you don't pay attention, things may change that will affect your bottom line—your grades.

On the first day of class, don't be psyched out by your professor. However, don't make an unrealistic expectation of your abilities as a student. Every college has difficult classes and easy classes. Your first semester should be a time for you to be "testing the waters" of your college or university. That means, no matter how much you would like to: don't take that multivariate calculus class and stay away from honors physics. This advice doesn't apply to everyone. However, if studying stresses you out, it probably will apply to you. On the other side of the coin, there are some professors who try to scare people out of their classes. They do this because they like small class sizes, and they are usually into the liberal arts. This type of class has the possibility of being an easy A because the professor thinks that you have stuck with the program and gave visible effort.

However, in general, a student should pay very close attention to these professors' attitudes, and the student should mimic the professor's ideas in papers and back them up. This validates these professors' views and makes you a better student in their eyes because it means you've paid attention in class. Follow this advice at your own risk! I only had three "C's" in college and the one I got in a liberal arts class was totally avoidable. I argued against the views of the English professor because I happened to think his views were poppycock, and I got slammed for it. After learning from that experience, I took a class with a professor whose views differed completely from mine; however, I wanted a good grade so I argued his arguments very well, and I got the "A". Try to find out the reputation of the course and of the professor before you get into the class. In general, your fellow students will give you a good picture of what you are getting into.

On the first day of class, don't go up to someone in your class and say "Hi! My name is Bob, and I have manic depression!" That just isn't starting off on the right foot. Let people get to know you, and then when you know they like you for who you are, you can let them know about a diagnosis you have. This way, they are much more likely to keep talking to you and be your friend. It is a strategy I've used as an undergrad and grad. Not everyone will react positively, there is the occasional jerk; however, most people will be understanding if you do it this way. Their rationale will be "Nobody's perfect." However, that is some time from the first class. You don't want them to see you as a diagnosis, you want them to see you as a person.

You want to take notes the first day of class. Note taking is an important skill in college, and many times tests come straight from the notes. Some people like to tape record the professor. I've thought of doing this, but I never got around to it. I just write down, in my own words, the concepts the professor is covering, and I try to get everything down. That way if he says he covered something in the notes, I'll have no excuse not to have the information. However, in some classes note taking is boring and useless. Why would that ever be? I've had classes where the professor would talk for hours about things that he or she wouldn't test us on. Why go to class in these situations? Sometimes attendance is part of the grade. However, if you feel that the professor is wasting your time, they probably are, and you shouldn't feel bad about missing a class or two. In my freshman year I went weeks without attending a calculus class because I found the professor confusing. However, even in this calculus class, the first few weeks of class were mandatory. If you didn't attend the first three classes, they'd drop you from the class. When in doubt, go to class.

Chapter 3: Your First Semester

Financial aid is one of the most stressful aspects of a college life. You have to check and re-check with them to make sure that there isn't some problem that needs your attention. For example, if the financial aid office sends you a letter, and you never receive it, you are still obligated to do what they ask or your financial aid may never get realized, and you'll have to drop out of college. To remedy this, check back with them maybe once a month, even if you think you have nothing to do. This way, you are covering for their mistakes. It may sound paranoid, but trust me this is the best way to do things. You don't want to miss out on an education because of an administrative problem.

Pace yourself your first semester. Don't take too many classes. Be realistic. Study constantly and don't cram. Each semester is long. You don't want to take too many classes because then you'll have less time to devote to getting each class. You have to be realistic about these things. They say that you need to study four hours each week for each credit to get an "A" in a class. This means if you are taking a four hour introductory math class, you'll need to log sixteen hours per week on that class to get an "A". I did not find this to be true in my case. I've gotten "As" in classes I only studied for four hours a week. On the other hand, I've had classes that I logged 20+ hours per week for four credits and I only got a B+, so it depends on the class. If you study constantly throughout the semester you won't have to cram. This means you won't have to pull all nighters. That is a good thing.

Getting into the routine of being a college student is a pleasant experience. There is nothing quite like the college experience. Socially, you will make friends. Intellectually, you'll break new ground. You'll probably get into a routine of eating with friends, and you'll probably also study with friends, just to encourage each other in your academic pursuits. On the other hand, there is the typical freshman. All they do is party and drink. If you do this, you can be rest assured that your grades will go down the drain, and probably all your friends' grades will too. I ask you: why go to a college, just to be kicked out?

Socializing on campus is almost a necessity. Some campuses even have "commuter lounges" for people who don't live on campus. People can't study all the time and not socialize because we are not machines. Making friends on campus is great because you can talk about things that are going on in the world and on campus. Academically, friends advanced in your same program of study can warn you about pitfalls in your way and which professors to avoid or take. That's insider information, and the SEC won't put you in jail for using that information. If you are in a class with a friend, you can even split the work. That way, you do half the work you'd ordinarily do, and it works out well for many classes.

Don't slack off! I've known very bright people who have done A work in the beginning of the semester, just to totally slack off at the end to get a D overall for the class. If you are going to work hard, try to do it just before finals, because the finals are usually weighed most heavily in your final grade. Not slacking off goes hand in hand with pacing yourself. If you make it a habit to study when you get a chance, you'll do much better on the tests. If you only cram for tests, you aren't giving the information time to settle and mature in your mind. This can really damage your chances of passing classes, forget about doing well.

Getting phone numbers of classmates is a good way to break the ice, and chances are if you miss a class you can get class notes from one of your phone buddies and vice-versa. This is very good because even missing one class puts you behind in the grand scheme of things. Splitting work with newfound friends in classes is a good way to go as well. This is especially true for liberal arts classes, I've found. Obviously there are books that must be read; however, if additional reading would make for a better grade, telling your friends, "Ok, you do a bit of research on Shakespeare, and I'll do the Donne." Then when you share your notes on that class, you are educating yourself above and beyond what is necessary. This will be reflected in your grade, in a positive manner.

The library. The best students I knew spent a lot of time studying in the library. The library is a good place to research things that you are studying, to get more depth of knowledge. Or, you can get away from a noisy roommate (or residence hall) to be able to focus more on your books. Alternatively, you can meet people there and make it a social occasion by mixing studying with socializing. I spent a lot of time with new thoughts and friends at the library as an undergraduate. I just couldn't study at my residence hall, no matter how hard I tried, because my bed was very inviting for naps. People would knock on my door to be social. Not that there is anything wrong with that, but if you are trying to concentrate, that doesn't help. Or, I'd wander around to see what people were doing.

I did very well, but I had a breakdown during the middle of my second semester back. It was already a month and a half into the semester so I withdrew from the courses I was still enrolled in and I went home. As soon as I could, I put the pieces back together. I started commuting to work on Stony-brook Campus from New York City which was a three hour trip each way, and I enrolled in twelve credits the next semester, taking care to choose easy classes. I felt heavily medicated the next semester, but I made it with over a 3.0 GPA. So, I was happy about that. After that horrible experience I knew I need-ed to take easy classes to graduate, so I became an English major and resolved to enjoying the rest of my college days.

A year goes by, and I get healthier every day and my dose of Navane gets lower every month, until I am no longer on any anti-psychotic drugs. Three days later, I am having my second psychotic break and I am in the hospital. I was tak-ing biology for dummies, Buddhism, two education classes, and one easy literature class. This break happened during the middle of the semester, so it was harder to pick up the pieces. My biology teacher just gave me an A- because that was the average I had while attending, so I had an easy time with her, thank goodness. My Buddhism professor let me take the final over the winter break, so I got my B there. The education professors were very understanding and gave me high grades. That was nice. The literature professor was a bit more harsh because I was kind of disrespectful to him during the term because I thought he repeated himself too often. So, he made me sweat, but he turned my incomplete into a B. So, I got out allright. The trick to getting all of these classes taken care of was that immediately after being discharged from the hospi-tal I went back to school to get my incompletes taken care of. I was a pit bull and wouldn't let go of my classes until they were resolved. The final semester I was able to finish commut-ing from New York City to Stonybrook, Long Island because there was only one class and it was an independent study so I didn't even have to go every week.

The key to academic survival during a psychotic break is to keep trying and don't give up on your classes. Chances are you'll not have wasted your time. Also, professors are very open-minded individuals most of the time and will give you the grade you deserve. So don't give up! You'll know in the future what to avoid to make sure that you will do better in school and what will trigger your psychosis. This knowledge will make you a more capable student and will, in the long run, save you a lot of headaches.

Come back as a fighter, with new wisdom!

Chapter 5: The saga continues

After your first semester, the thing is that you need to keep your momentum going and not slack off in classes. The question arises: "How do I avoid burning myself out?" The answer to that is simple, yet complex. The simple part is that you need to keep choosing subjects that are interesting to you. Selecting subjects you wouldn't mind studying is your best bet to long-term success in your academics. Your worst mistake would be to choose a lot of math courses if you can't stand numbers. No matter how driven you are, that is a sure way of dampening your resolve.

Usually, college will take a full time student four years to complete. That means for four years of your life you need to be psyched about what you are studying and keeping focused on the end result. For people with a mental illness it could take much longer than the four years. That's ok though. Just getting a college degree is a major milestone in a healthy person's life. How much more sweet is it to the person with the mental disability! It is telling the mental disability, "You do not own me! I am greater than you are!" It is an affirmation of self that should not be forgotten.

Each objective you achieve in your quest for an education is a major milestone. You should take time out to celebrate the good fortune you have after each and every major accomplishment. Don't be too hard on yourself! When I got my Masters in Library Science, even though I couldn't afford it, I bought a class ring. I thought it was something I needed to do to respect the fact that I had made it that far. When I took the GRE, I bought myself a Ralph Lauren Polo dress shirt. I don't wear it often anymore, but every time I do, I feel proud to be wearing it because it means something to me.

You need to be patient with yourself, because if you blow your stack at every little thing, chances are you won't do as well as if you tried to keep your cool. For example, I had a professor at Library School that called us a "bunch of dorks" for not following instructions to the T. So, I thought he was going to lower my grade on one particular test from an A- to a C+. Needless to say this made me very upset. It was with this in mind that I approached this professor, in a polite manner. I was surprised when he told me "Not to worry." In the end, I got an A+ in the class for both my test scores and my participation in class, and my polite approach was the way to go. If I had exploded at this professor, I can imagine what would have happened to my career as a librarian: it would have gone down the drain. Restraint is a virtue for the person with mental illness, and believe me it is rewarded.

Keeping the end in sight is always the way to go. Whenever you don't think it is going to be worth it, just remember that winners never quit and quitters never win. If you fall down seven times, you should get up eight times to prove you are stronger than your circumstances. Looking back at all the tests I had to overcome in school due to my mental illness, I am satisfied since I did my best and that is a comfort to me.

Another thing that has helped me in life, not just in school is that I can distance myself from my psychosis when the psychosis is just beginning, and I know when to medicate myself. I have insight and it is a good thing to have. I am not in denial that I am mentally ill, I work through it and by understanding it better I have more control over it. If I said to myself, "There is nothing wrong with me." I'd be a bigger fool than Big Bird. However, if I learn the signs that my mental illness is coming upon me then I can adapt to these signs and manage them better.

Chapter 6: Graduation

Graduation! Graduation is one of the best times in a person's life. It is the ending of life being a student, and a beginning of life as a contributing member of society. The graduation ceremony is not a useless thing. It commemorates the effort and hard work that were needed to get you to this place in your life. It's only natural to step back and take the honors that will be bestowed on you on behalf of the university or college you have attended. Take it with pride, even if, like me, you can't wake up early enough to attend the ceremony!

So, what now? Well, there are generally two options open to those who graduate from college: get a job, or go back to school. Since most people who get an advanced degree are advanced in age this may or may not be an option for you. In the past, getting a job, other than a job that was volunteer in nature was impossible for many with mental illness. However, President Clinton in 1999 passed a law that, eventually, allowed people with mental illness to work and have their dignity. Whatever you might want to say about the man, don't say that he wasn't a friend to those with mental illness! He was, because he opened a door that was shut for far too long. Thank you Mr. Clinton! It is now up to the states to adopt this law in their own.

Thank you for reading my book. If you enjoyed it, won't you please take a moment to leave me a review?

Sincerely Yours,
Will Jiang

Discover other titles by William Jiang, MLS

- Guide to Natural Mental Health
- Tackling French The Easy Way
- Tackling Spanish The Easy Way
- Tackling Portuguese The Easy Way
- Inglés Fácilmente
- A Historical Reader: The New York Times and Madness, 1851-1922
- La guía del Bibliotecario Médico: Ansiedad, Depresión, Bipolar, y Esquizofrenia: Nutrición y Terapias Complementarias, Jorge Alvarado, Translator
- Entre la Esquizofrenia y Mi Voluntad: Una Historia de Locura y Esperanza (Spanish Edition) Jorge Alvarado, Translator

Facebook Group: Living Well With Schizophrenia
Author Blog: http://www.mentalhealthbooks.net